Cultural Diversity in Health and Social Care

Some Questions and Answers for Health Care Professionals

Nevel A. Vassel, Ph.D.

About the Author
Nevel A. Vassel, Ph.D. (Manchester)

Dr Nevel Vassel, who has roots in Jamaican culture, specialises in Multicultural, Diversity Health and Social Care Issues, Multicultural Staff Training and Development and Leadership and Mentoring. He has over 20 years of lecturing experience in Further and Higher Education institutions on a variety of courses such as Cultural Issues in Health Care, Educational Management, Health Education, Classroom Management, Evidence Based Research, Project Management for Nurses, and Mentoring. He has presented academic papers at national and international conferences in the United Kingdom, Jamaica, USA, and Oslo, Norway, India (Chennai, Kerala, and New Delhi) and has worked in Kerala, India and Macedonia University, Greece. He is Senior Lecturer and Route Director in Ethnic and Cultural Diversity in Health and Social Care at Birmingham City University, United Kingdom.

Copyright

ISBN 978-1-4475-1601-9

Foreword by Professor Gajendra K. Verma

This is an important and stimulating book, which contain discussions and important issues the nature of racism, ethnicity and multiculturalism. Dr. Vassel's ideal of a multicultural health care delivery system, which rises above the ideologies of racism may seem idealistic but is not an impossible dream. I admire the integrity of Dr. Vassel's scholarship, and of his commitment to the values of inter-culturalism. The reader will benefit from the ethical and spiritual insights contained within the case vignettes of multicultural health care delivery. This book is a valuable addition to the literature of multiculturalism, and I commend it to a wide readership.

Gajendra Verma, Emeritus Professor of Education, Former Dean of Research and Graduate School, University of Manchester

Foreword by Professor Christopher R. Bagley

Nevel Vassel, a doyen of Jamaican culture as well as a noted scholar. In the present text, he brings a rich cultural insight and humanity to bear on delivering health services to minorities in general and to African Caribbean community members in particular. In past years he has reached out to cultures in the Indian Sub-Continent, and has developed fruitful collaboration in teaching and research with several Indian universities. This collaboration has given him fresh insights and links with the South Asian community in Britain. I particularly enjoyed Dr. Vassel's focus on religion and spiritual issues in this text, and their implications for health care delivery. Religious or not, the reader will greatly benefit from his analysis and polemic.

Christopher R. Bagley,
Emeritus Professor of Social Science, University of Southampton;

ACKNOWLEDGEMENT

I would like to extend my sincere thanks and appreciation to Gajendra Verma, Emeritus Professor of Education and to Christopher Bagley, Emeritus Professor of Social Science; for their invaluable advice in the development this book. My heartfelt appreciation to all those who have encouraged me to write this book. Thanks to my family for their continuous practical and moral support and for their encouragement.

CONTENTS   PAGES

SECTION 1:   RACISM, CULTURE AND DIVERSITY ISSUES

work place

SECTION 2: MULTICULTURAL HEALTCARE: CASE STUDIES

SECTION 3: ILLNESSES, SPIRITUALITY, BELIEFS

SECTION 4:   DIABETIS, SEXUAL HEALTH MENTAL HEALTH

INTRODUCTION

This Volume arises from my lectures and seminars on multiculturalism and health. Frequently students (mainly health care workers) asked questions relating to health and culture, so I decided to systematise this process, asking students to list their most salient questions. The questions below are a selection of the most significant, interesting and challenging of the issues addressed.

SECTION 1: RACISM, CULTURE AND DIVERSITY ISSUES

1.1   What do we understand by the term 'Race'?

The concept of race is one of the most difficult terms to define since biologists, anthropologists, social scientists and other disciplines have given their own definitions within their subject areas. Macionis and Plummer (2008) suggested that the term 'race' is a very muddled 'even dangerous' concept, but can be referred to a category of people who share biologically transmitted traits, that members of society deem socially significant. The Oxford English Dictionary defines "race" as a large group of people with common ancestry and inherited physical features.

In addition, King and Stansfield, (1990) dictionary of genetics, defines race as: ''A phenotypically and/or geographically distinctive sub specific group, composed of individuals inhabiting a defined geographical and/or ecological region, and possessing characteristic phenotypic and gene frequencies that distinguish it from other such groups". From a biological perspective, Gillborn (1990) documents that during the nineteenth century, biologists used the term 'race' to place human beings in apparently distinct groups (types) thought to share a common biological ancestry, even referring to "the English race" as distinct from "the Welsh race" and so on. The difference in physical features such as skin colour gave birth to the most virulent ideologies alleging genetic inferiority of certain races. Giddens (2001) recalled the work of Count Joseph Arthur de Gobineau (1816-1882) on the grouping of races into three distinctive sets: white (Caucasian) black (Negroid) and yellow (Mongoloid). In addition, according to Haralambos and Holborn, (2004) observed that Morton (1839) based his argument on the measurement of skulls to distinguished five races, which are as follows; Caucasian (from Europe, India, parts of North Africa and the Middle East), Mongolian (Chinese and Eskimos), Malay (from Malaysia and the Polynesian Island), American (Native American from North and South America) and Ethiopian (from sub-Saharan Africa). An earlier explanation of this concept is forward by Verma and Ashworth (1986), that the concept of race was designed to categorise people by their physical characteristics (e.g. colour of skin, texture of hair, shape of skull, nose or cheekbones). These ideas led to the categorisation of five racial groups as described by physical and medical anthropologists: In this nomenclature, even very dark-skinned people from India such as Tamils are classified as Caucasian. 'Caucasian' is *not,* in anthropological terminology, synonymous with

2

being 'white'.

Billington etal (1998) notes that 'Race' is not scientific, but a cultural construct. Ideologically, this concept has been used by dominant group to justify various types of exploitation, including slavery, force labour, sexual coercion, segregation and lack of civil rights such as voting and education. However, it is clear that there is no such thing as a clear racial group, in genetic terms. All of us are the result of multiple ancestors, some of them fair-skinned, some of them dark-skinned. In both genetic (i.e. biological) and social terms skin colour should, strictly speaking, be no more significant than is hair-colour or eye-colour. The largest biological differences in human populations are not those between 'races', but those between genders.

The notion of race from a biological perspective has been discredited (Gillborn, 1990; Verma and Ashworth 1986). These writers argued that the concept of 'race' is more meaningful when translated into 'ethnicity', now including factors such as language, religion, moral values, customs, dress styles and nutrition. Groups can be 'racialised' when the negative stereotypes associated with racialism are imposed on a group. For example, the racist epithet "Pakis" incorporates a number of negative attitudes and stereotypes about anyone with cultural origins in the Indian sub-continent.

Banton's (1987) describes the various attempts to divide human beings into different biological or racial groups and developed the hypothesis that as part of society's negative attitudes, 'race' is divided into three categories: race as lineage, race as a type and race as a sub-species. According to Banton (1987) race as lineage reflects a 'single race' idea, arguing that humans belong to a single species of origin. It was believed that as human beings migrated around the world distinctive lineages developed. It is the belief that due to exposure to different environmental conditions, that human-beings developed variation in their physical appearance – but these differences relate to superficial external features due to adaptation to different climates. Oppenheimer, (2006) argued that beneath the skin, all human beings are virtually the same. Recent genetic studies confirm this idea, showing that the ancestors of all human beings almost certainly came 'out of Africa' around 100,000 years ago

Race as sub-category stems from the viewpoint of the combination between 'race as lineage' and 'race as a type', (Banton, 1987). This concept is derived from the work of Charles Darwin (1859). According to Banton, the idea draws on the notion that members of the same species (e.g. homo sapiens) can all interbreed and produce offspring, but for evolutionary adaption, changes may result in different groups. This results in sub-species, which may have different characteristics but are all member of the same family group, and are capable of fertile intermarriage, which is increasingly common in today's globally networked world. In many southern states in United States of America (as in apartheid South Africa) there were laws against 'miscegenation' banning marriages between 'whites' and individuals with one-sixteenth African ancestry.

This notion of race highlights a biological expression of phenotypically defined genetic inheritance.

This idea of separate racial phenotypes breaks down when one considers a culture such as Jamaica, whose motto is "Out of many, one people". Thus Jamaicans are descended of a mixture of the original Caribs and Awarak (Amerindians), 'Maroons' African slaves, white slave owners and overseers, Asian Indian labourers and merchants, and Jewish and Chinese traders. Genetic analysis of an individual Jamaican using DNA illustrates this multiple heritage - a good example is the world champion hurdler Colin Jackson, who in the BBC series "Who do think you are?" (Barratt, 2008), was reported to have a genetic mixture of Amerindian (7%), African (55%) and European (38%) ancestry. The commentator noted that Jackson had mid- to light-brown skin, somewhat Europeanised features but also some facial appearance reminiscent of his Amerindian forbears. Colin Jackson is one of many world-beating athletes from this small island, which is also a culturally powerful force in world music. These creative and powerful individuals have emerged from a culture in which 'racial mixing' has been a norm for several generations. The notion of race prior to research by geneticists was based on the ideology that all human beings did not share similar origins and that humanity was divided into distinctive groups, some superior to others.

Modern research has shown that this idea is, scientifically speaking, false. Cavalli-Sforza (2000) in his monumental study of *Genes, Peoples and*

Languages concluded from DNA analysis of a large series from all of the main countries of the world, that "the variation between two random individuals within any one population is 85 percent as large as that between two individuals randomly selected from the world's population." In other words, DNA analysis fails to distinguish, in 85 percent of cases, between people of allegedly different racial origins; DNA differences within any particular ethnic group are approximately similar to those between ethnic groups. This finding leads Cavalli-Sforza to conclude that: "It seems wise to me, therefore, to abandon any attempt at racial classification along traditional lines, the intellectual interest of a rational classification of races clashes with the absurdity of imposing an artificial discontinuity on a phenomenon that is very clearly continuous."

The continuity of 'racial' classification is obvious to a visitor to the Caribbean or to India — both of these regions include people with light brown skin as well as very dark skin, and a variety of facial features and hair types. Furthermore, as Cavalli-Sforza shows, the continuing pressures to find marriage partners outside of one's immediate kinship group means that people with different DNA ancestries are constantly being absorbed. Increasing international migration means that mixed marriages of very type are becoming increasingly common. As Platt (2009) showed with her British research, the rate of mixed marriages in Britain among African-Caribbean groups is high, with more than 40 percent of African-Caribbean's being in marital partnership with someone of white, European descent. Perhaps multicultural Britain should adopt the Jamaican motto: "Out of many, one people".

1.2   What do we mean by 'White Supremacy'?

White supremacy thrives on the artificial notion that differences observed between 'races' illustrate the superiority of whites over groups, such as African Americans (Coker 2001). Historical research claimed that Caucasians had the largest cranial capacity, and Ethiopian the smallest, resulting in the former being more intellectual and far more advanced than sub-Sahara Africans (Haralambos and Holborn 2004). The artificial idea of race has also been used by Europeans to create a social, political and class hierarchy. For example, Miller (2002) pointed out that following emancipation in Jamaica, social structure was determined by race and colour in the post-slavery, colonial era. At the top of the hierarchy ladder were 'whites', including all persons of European ancestry followed, by 'brown' or 'fair' people colloquially called mulatto, and lastly Black descendants who were persons of African ancestry. Only after Jamaica's independence have these rigid barriers begun to crumble.

In Europe Adolf Hitler and the German Nazis excoriated and virtually exterminated Jews and Gypsies of Central Europe on racial grounds, despite the patent lack of hereditary phenotypical differences between Germans and other 'races'. The pseudo-science which placed Aryans at the pinnacle of a racial hierarchy, justifying the killing and enslavement of Jews, Gypsies and Slavs is now utterly discredited. Nevertheless, Gypsies and Roma people remain persecuted groups across Europe today. Nothing terrifies a middle class white enclave in Britain more, than to have gypsies encamp close by. Hitler also murdered homosexuals in the death camps, and gay people are still "a race apart" persecuted in Africa, the Middle East, and by many Christian churches

Notions of racial superiority were used by Christopher Columbus to enslave, murder and extinguish the Arawak Indians of the Caribbean (Jamaica), just as later Colonial powers in Canada and Australia hunted down and killed to the last child, the native populations of Newfoundland and Tasmania. The European slave traders - the English, Spanish, Portuguese, Dutch and their American counterparts - used ideas of racial superiority as justification for continuing the African slave trade for over 400 years. Many fortunes were made in Britain through the horrors of slavery, and the prosperity of cities such as Bristol and Liverpool owed much to the trade in slaves.

The Apartheid system was developed by Afrikaners (originally Calvinist 'refugees' from Dutch tolerance – see Bagley, 1973) who discriminated profoundly against the indigenous of South Africans, as well as against 'coloureds' (unions of white and black people). The argument of racial inferiority was used to justify oppression that was clearly in the economic interests of the white settlers.

According to Kush (1983), David Hume, the famous British philosopher wrote in his *Essays and Treaties on Several Subject* (1753) that there "... never was a civilised nation of any other complexion than white, nor even any individual

8

eminent either in action or speculation." Further examples on how race has been used in a degrading way are cited by Kush – for example, the statements made by the famous French historian Charles Seignobos (1938) alleging that all civilised people belong to the white race, while people of other races had remained savage or barbarian, like men of prehistoric times.

The notion of white supremacy expresses itself through in the actions of prejudice, stereotyping, victimising, discrimination, isolation, exclusion, division and segregation. White supremacy can lead to the situation where white cultural values and the state of being white are imagined to be the norm, and any variation from this norm is automatically viewed as problematic or pathological (Lago, 2006). White supremacy is kept alive through organised systems such as institutional racism, including systems of colonisation. It can be expressed in behavioural terms such as the cultural aggression, cultural piracy and cultural genocide that have been committed against majority of people of colour by the white European group. White supremacy involves the control of fundamental building blocks for society in terms of finance, legal values and beliefs which are used to place another culture, society, 'race' or community at major disadvantage.

White supremacy goes against the notion of equal opportunity, self-sufficiency, self-productivity and self-reliance. It promotes a dependency culture, and as Madhubuti (2009) argues, "We" (the Black community) are dependent upon the white community for material things that are life giving and life saving including water, food, jobs, energy, education, politics, health care, drugs, transportation, culture and values, law and order and religion. Furthermore white supremacist ideology is expressed through capitalism and imperialism, including under-education of the black man leading to unemployment and underemployment (Madhubuti 2009). In the Marxist model, the racialised groups occupy the role of "the reserve army of labour" in the capitalist economy.

Gillborn (2005) expounds the idea that white supremacy assumes the ideology that white people deserve to have the major share of the resources of power in Western capitalist societies. He also draws on Ansley's (1997) interpretation of white supremacy as one in which the self consciousness of racist and white supremacist groups assumes an overwhelming part of their self-consciousness. In its more subtle form, a diluted form of white supremacist ideology defines (in terms of "institutional racism") political, economic and cultural systems in which whites overwhelmingly control power and material resources, and conscious or unconscious ideas of white superiority. Ideas of white dominance and non-white subordination are daily re-enacted across a broad array of institutions and social settings. The starting point for white supremacy is through the colour of whiteness - an ethnic description for non-melanin people. Reflecting on this, Leonardo (2002) argues that ideologies of 'whiteness' form a racial discourse. Bonnett (1997) suggests that ideologies of whiteness have developed over the past two hundred years in western societies as taken-for-granted experiences, structured upon a varying set of supremacist assumptions (sometimes cultural, sometimes biological, sometimes moral, sometimes all three). Non-white identities, by contrast, have been denied the privileges of being normatively part of western culture, and are marked within the West as marginal and inferior.

Gillborn (2005) in his paper on"Education policy as an act of white supremacy: whiteness, critical race theory and education reform" outlines the meaning of terminology from an anti-racist perspective that promotes a different view of white supremacy than the limited model usually denoted by the term in everyday language. He argues that white supremacy is a term usually reserved for individuals, organisations and philosophies that are overtly and self-consciously racist in the most crude and obvious way. All white groups such as British National Party (BNP) and the Ku Klux Klan (KKK), aligned themselves with the philosophical belief that they are superior to people of colour, and deserve their privileged position because they belong to a superior race. However, according to Kennedy (2010) the BNP was court ordered to comply with the Race relations law in Britain resulting in amended of their constitution to allow black and Asian people to become members.

In Britain from an organisational perspective, racial superiority practices came to light when the death of Steven Lawrence initiated a major enquiry published as the McPherson report (1999), which identified the British police as 'institutionally racist'. Also in the educational services, Bernard Coard a known educational and political activist

11

wrote in the 1970s, that the British school system was responsible for 'making the West Indian child educationally sub-normal' through a process of discrimination and negative labelling (Coard, 1971). In addition, Griffiths and Hope (2000) highlighted the Swan Report (1985) which provided sound research information that racism had a causal effect on the educational experience of black children in United Kingdom

Vassel (2006) argues that ideologies of white superiority promote Euro-centric attitudes. Yurugu (1994) argues further that the manifestation of Euro-centrism as a belief system influences white thinking, for example the idea of white power as domination over others, rather than as power as creative capacity to act in positive ways. Akbar also examines the impact of negative beliefs about dark skin colour compared with white, skin on certain groups. Akbar (1996) observes that many African American continue to assume that beauty, competence and worth are far greater in those with the most Caucasian feature. There are still vast sums of money spent yearly on skin lighteners, hair straighteners and wigs, in the vain effort to change African American physical features. This may be described as "the Michael Jackson syndrome". The 'Colour Meanings Test' (CMT); and 'Pre-School Racial Attitudes Measure' (PRAM), developed in America have shown that many African American children preferred the colour white, and rated images of white children more favourably than their own ethnic group (Williams and Weed, 2004). In an extensive cross-cultural study using these measures in young children from different ethnic backgrounds in Canada, Britain, rural Jamaica and rural Ghana,

Bagley and Young (1988) showed complex patterns. White children had the most bias in favour of white figures, and in rural Jamaica black children also had a significant white bias, as did black children in Britain. But Ghanaian children showed very little bias in favour of white figures, suggesting that in a culture which sees being black as natural and unremarkable, these incipient racial biases do not exist. Moreover, children of Ghanaian immigrants to Canada retained their lack of colour bias. Wilson (1990) sums up the beliefs about colour of many white individuals, as historically providing the emotional and cognitive support for the murder or slavery of millions of people, plundering, pillage, and the ravage of thousands of hamlet, villages, towns, cities, states and nations in Africa and elsewhere. Wilson shows that for the ruling class (and for those who supported this class) of the white nations, the support for policies of repression are newspapers and books, media which through misrepresentation, omissions and lies justified the painful reality of the truly murderous trek across the globe - permitting the colonialists and their heirs to think of themselves as inherently good, and their victims as inherently evil (Wilson 1990). Wilson's account captures the events of colonisation, enslavement, promotion of national self interest, criminalising a race, and instigating and maintaining to this day, world poverty in respect to the most African countries. These ideologies still have sway amongst the Western elites, through such institutions as the World Bank, and the International Monitory Fund (IMF) who organise terms of trade for the primary benefit of their white race.

1.3 Is racism a personal attitude problem or a culture-centred problem?

Haralambos and Holborn (2004) referred to the Solomon (1993) notion of racism as ideologies and social processes which discriminate against other on the basis of their punitively differently racial membership. Furthermore, Macionis and Plummer (2002) states that it is a powerful and destructive form of prejudice, based on the belief that one racial category is innately superior or inferior to another. The issue of racism can reflect personal problems or individual psychological dispositions; or it can be a culturally socialised disposition; or both. Gidden (2002) explanation of psychological disposition of an individual focus on the fact that it begins with prejudice operates through the use of stereotype thinking and the person(s) draws on stereotype and vent their antagonism against people blaming them for things that are not their fault. Blaut (1992) make clear that within cultural racist theory, 'white' is no longer the superior 'race' but rather European the superior culture. Non-Europeans are thereby defined as inferior in attained levels of achievement, and not in potential for achievement, thus distinguishing cultural racism from earlier forms of racism.

In functional terms, racism seeks to suppress the right of other people to enjoy the freedom accorded to a dominant group; usually the dominant group is white. Resting on the notion of white supremacy reinforced in some cases, by centuries of political and economic power which it has wielded over the years, the dominant group ruthlessly guards its privileges and advantages (Verma 1986). Moreover, racism begins with the need of one people to exploit another and the development of the ideology to justify this exploitation (Carew 1988). In addition, Hicks (1981) suggested that racism involves three basic belief components. These are (a) the myth that human kinds consist of well-defined races; (b) some races are superior to others; and (c) the superior races should rule over inferior races. In deciding the distinction between allegedly higher and lower 'races', the Europeans as military conquerors set themselves as the highest group in this supposed hierarchy of race Bradley (1991 p.xxi).

Furthermore, racism is one of the factors that has caused profound and chronic social and educational disadvantage, affecting ethnic minority groups in Britain (Singh 1993). Racism does not, of course, move tidily and unchanged through time and history. It assumes new forms and articulates new antagonisms in different settings. Coker (2001) argued that racism is one of the most difficult and painful words used in the English language. It is a word that inspires fear, anger and revulsion in equal measure from all manner of people. For example, Parsia (2005) has observed that the term 'Pakis' is considered by many Pakistanis, particularly in Great Britain, to be offensive; and observed that "Most Americans are unaware of the sensitivity of the term." In addition, Chun et al (1983) observed that racism is institutional in nature, and is maintained by society through a variety of social institutions, to form "institutional racism".

Responding therefore to the original question, racism can be embedded in a person's attitude that disrespects ethnic minorities as human beings. It forms a set of beliefs and ideologies that can fuel hate, rage, segregation, isolation, victimisation and stereotyping of the identified group, based on the false belief that the white race is superior, and those of colour are inferior (Pettigrew, 1979). In addition racism may be seen as a corruption of the mind, and of the decent impulses which should stem from basic humanity. The ideology of white supremacy is not merely a pattern of individual and/or institutional practice; it is a universally operating 'system' of white supremacy. For the racist, to exert dominance over ethnic minorities must involve planned strategies to divide and rule, colonise, and stereotype, creating acts of cultural and physical genocide, creating religious, political and economic biases aimed at fostering the continued privileged position of their own "race". Tools such as education, religion, law, warfare and media are used both overtly and covertly to justify and carry out racist practices.

Ridley (1995) argues that racism always involves harmful behaviour; many rituals of racism occur in private, in ways which are difficult to change. Racism is learnt in the same manner as many operant behaviours are learned. Racism is responsible for creating racist ideologies which underlie, or reflect, a variety of assumptions about minority or "inferior" groups. Racist opinions can infect the thinking of individuals who we suppose should have been enlightened by their general rationality. Thus David Hume, the 'father of British philosophy' is known for his profoundly racist views – quoted by Kush (1983) from Hume's book *Essays and Treaties on Several* Subject Vol. 1, London (1753): 'I am apt to suspect Negroes to be naturally inferior to white. There has never been a civilised nation of any complexion than white or even any individual eminent either in action or speculation. No ingenious manufacturers amongst them, no arts, no sciences (Hume 1753). As Morton (2002) shows, this racism was not only general for Hume's time, but may also have slowed campaigns to abolish slavery. The legacy of Hume's prejudice infected Victorian ideas of colonialism, modern ideas of colonial dependence, and the ideology of the rightness of rule by the European powers in Asia, Africa and the Americas.

Racism modulates its form: the targets of racism change and the institutions of racism become more subtle, even though prejudice remains virulent. Research by Craig (2009) suggested that although the targets of racism may have changed somewhat, the proportions holding xenophobic or racist attitudes have not substantially changed in the past 30 years. Today in Britain the most targeted groups are so-called "asylum seekers" and refugees. Islamophobia is the new racism in Britain (Al-Refai and Bagley, 2008; Rowntree Trust, 2009). The MacPherson Enquiry (1999) into the racist murder of Stephen Lawrence in the late 1990s described a "culture of systemic racism" which infected many British institutions – a conclusion similar to that reached by MacDonald in 1989. The maintenance of institutional racism is not part of overt racism, but is part of a general system of prejudiced attitudes subtly and perhaps unconsciously held. In education this can be seen at work in the exclusion figures: youth of African

Caribbean descent are three times more likely than European-descent youth to be excluded from school for alleged learning or behavioural problems (Wanless, 2006; Strand, 2008) – similar findings to those made by Coard (1971). Teachers, through biased perception, often "mark down" African Caribbean pupils in exam settings (Burgess, 2010). Institutional racism may also infect health care settings, as a Department of Health enquiry found following the investigation of the death "under section" of an African Caribbean patient (DH, 2005).

1.4   The meaning of 'culture'

The idea of culture can be expressed as the global identity of a group of people resulting from shared values, belief, norms and other characteristics within a society, or political framework - an identity that is relatively stable and is transmitted or nurtured between generations. The United Kingdom includes not only the cultures represented by the three constituent countries (England, Scotland and Wales) and its Principality (Northern Ireland) but within each country of the UK there are many cultural groups reflecting a diverse religious and migrant history. Culture can be described as a body of learned behaviours that is passed from generation to generation, society to society, individual to individual, community to community. Macions and Plummer (2002) state that sociologist define culture as *designs for living: the values, beliefs, behaviour, practices and material objects that constitute a people 'way of life'.* It is a social construct characterised by the behaviour and attitudes of social groups (Coker,

2001). It can be identified in the expression of religion, spirituality, music, art, dress, food and cleanliness rituals, medical practices and accounts of ethnic history. Cultural identity is dynamic in nature. Cultural identity is flexible and adaptable and helps to shape all relationships within the community.

Culture can be interpreted in differing ways by various role-holders and power brokers (including politicians), resulting in different interpretations of what culture means, and the degree to which it might be changed or respected. It can involve abstract belief, as well as everyday feelings and behaviour within one's cultural group. Culture can be practised within moral, ethical settings. Culture creates the pathway for individual identity. Cultural identity is variable and sometimes arbitrary - for example in Muslim society some types of deed are *haram* (forbidden); only the right (or dominant) hand is used for eating; and during the Holy Month of Ramadan no food or liquid is consumed during daylight hours. Also in Akan culture in Ghana, the use of the left hand in exchanges is regarding as acceptable behaviour (Koranteng 2008). In other societies such as Hindu culture, married women wear a *mangal sutra* (a necklace with pendant), generally given by the husband, strung on necklace of gold or black beades. Part of the cultural identity expressed by Rastafarians is observed through the wearing of the hair in dreadlock and uncut. (Kaur, 2001).

Cultures can be modified in the face of changes in the social environment and interactions with other cultural groups. But one's culture is not like a suit of clothing, which can be easily discarded or exchanged for each new lifestyle that comes along. It is like a security blanket and although it may appear to some to be worn and tattered, outmoded and even ridiculous, it often has great meaning to its owner (Spardley and McCurdy, 1974). Culture incorporates a set of guidelines (both explicit and implicit) which individuals acquire as members of a particular cultural group, and which informs them how they might view the world, how to experience it emotionally, and how to behave in relation to other people, what are supernatural forces, and what is the nature of the environment (Helman, 1997). Finally, it must be stressed that belonging to a cultural group is a voluntary status: it is wrong to assume a one-to-one correlation between a particular "racial" group (however defined) and any particular global identity. Individuals may choose, for example, to follow secular paths and identify wholly as British, Welsh, Scottish or Irish, or simply label themselves as a "human being" whose identity transcends national, ethnic and religious boundaries.

1.5   Multiculturalism, Diversity and Pluralism

Multiculturalism is a concept that emphasises the unique characteristics of different cultures in the world, especially as they relate to one another within defined political boundaries or states. The term was used in 1957 to describe the different language groups in Switzerland, and came into common currency in Canada in the late 1960s, and quickly spread to other English-speaking countries. (Spiritus Temporis 2005). Britain is considered to be a multicultural society, since the population consists of individuals or groups who have identified themselves (their primary or secondary identity) as African-Caribbean, African, Welsh, Gaelic Scots, Irish, Pakistani, Indian, Sikh, Jewish, Polish, English, Chinese, and many others; as well as various forms of religious and gender-orientation identities - each with a defined cultural identity, and shared rituals and languages. The United States of America is also considered to be a multicultural society because of the various ethnic groups who retain aspects of traditional language, religion and other customs. For example there are Hispanic, African American, Jewish, Irish, Italian, German, Scandinavian and many other groups. Each group may have their own religion, language, beliefs system, family life, and special ways of preparing food and diet. The celebration of key events - for example, death, birth, marriage, often varies from group to group. The uniqueness of the group when collectively studied is a key factor in describing multiculturalism. Multiculturalism, in its ideal form, can be classified as the positive interaction and mutual tolerance of these different cultures within a single national state.

Diversity is referred to as the circumstance of ethnic and other differences within a given population. A successfully diverse but inclusive society will encompass factors such as race, age, gender, sexual orientation, ethnicity, ability, religion, and spirituality, guaranteeing the safety and right to free expression of each group, encouraging mutual tolerance and respect between the groups. Moreover, diversity can also be described as differences in terms of various professional backgrounds of individuals, such as being teachers, lawyers, nurses, doctors with specialism or special fields of interest, and other blue and white collar workers with various special skills. Each individual occupies various combinations of roles and statuses, which make up an individual identity, or consciousness of self. How society perceives and evaluates individual identities may influence what Goffman (1963) calls "the presentation of the self in everyday life." Individuals with stigmatised identities (such being gay, or having a psychiatric illness) may result in extreme dilemmas for the individual (Bagley and Tremblay, 2001; Bagley and King, 2004).

Diversity can also be used to describe marital and parental status within a specific community. A mutually tolerant society encourages tolerant mixture, and one which should encourage recognition of ethnic value, personal identity and status, and religious differences (Verma et al. 1994). The complex interaction of individual statuses is found not only amongst communities, but also within the hierarchal structure of society. What is crucial is that one's birth status as an individual should not determine an individual's life chances. Unfortunately, Britain is still a class-ridden society, with imperfect patterns of upward mobility (Bagley, 2008). Thus the individual status of a child's parents is all too often a deterministic factor in the child's health, mortality risk as well as educational and occupational progress.

One of the problems of civil society in Britain is that sub-groups of individuals, who identify themselves by a particular ethnic, class, regional, religious or value orientation, may express overt hostility, or thinly disguised contempt, for each other. Class prejudice, prejudice against the uneducated or unemployed; against those with 'unpopular' regional accents (e.g. from Liverpool, Glasgow, Newcastle or Birmingham); prejudices within and between minority ethnic groups (e.g. against gay people, who are often fiercely condemned by members of African Caribbean and Muslim minority group members); the oft-expressed Christian contempt for gay people; and the continued antipathy between Catholic and Protestant, not only in Ulster but also in large cities of Irish settlement such as Liverpool and Glasgow. While Britain is a nation divided by petty prejudice, it is crucial that public services, such as the health care delivery system, set aside such prejudices. The health professional must treat all he or she meets as equal in need, demanding the utmost dedication in professional care.

Pluralism according to Macionis and Plummer (2002), suggested that the term is referred to categories of people who are social different, but share basic social resources more or less equally. It is a state in which racial and ethnic minorities are distinct but have social purity.

Pluralism is essentially a society centred, not state approach (Bilton 2002). Plus Marsh and Keating (2006) adds that it is a perspective usually associated with the study of politics or the media, which suggest that the institution of a democratic society are responsive to the diverse interest in that society. There are two types of pluralism, the first being *political pluralism*, which captures the ideological differences (political or religious) in a society which is culturally and ethnically homogenous. Marsh and Keating (2006) notes that this construct aims to embrace a number of sectional interest. Government responses are portrayed as a compromise between pluralities of influences. Power is spread across a wide range of social location; organisation representing various interest exists because no one interest group is allowed to dominate.

The second aspect of pluralism is *cultural pluralism*, which is identified by institutional and value separateness of ethnic and linguistic groups within the same society. Examples of cultural pluralism can be found in United States and Canada (Appleton 1983). Britain is considered to be a plural society which captures cultural diversity consisting of European (i.e. indigenous Britons), Indian, Pakistani, Bangladeshi, African-Caribbean, African, Chinese, Vietnamese, Irish, Welsh, Scottish and other groups. Within this plural society, most share a common linguistic and geographical heritage. For example, Vyas (1983) explains that the British Gujarat community may consist of orthodox Muslim and associated sects (Ismailis, Bohoras and Ishnasheris), a range of Hindu groups and a small number of Jains and Parsees. Despite this, contributors to the University Issue of the *Gujarat Samachar* were able to speak of the 'collective Gujarati consciousness' in Gujaratis settled in Britain. As British Gujaratis, they have added being British and speaking English as a first or second language to their complex identities.

Other salient examples are seen in the Jewish remembrance of The Holocaust, and numerous religious festivals; people of African Ancestry in the diaspora celebrating Black History Month; Muslims observing the fasting month of Ramadan;

and Hindus celebrating festivals such as Diwali; and new year celebrations in 'Chinatown' centres in large cities. Part of a complex plural society is the network of religious primary and secondary schools: about a third of British schools fall into this category, the large majority being 'voluntary aided' by state funds. Across Britain there are Anglican, Roman Catholic, Muslim, Quaker, Jewish, Hindu and Seventh Day Adventist schools catering for the educational needs of a variety of religious groups. All of these schools incorporate, through the National Curriculum, teaching on citizenship education in which children learn to understand, and be tolerant of, other ethnic and religious groups, as well as learning about being a 'good citizen' in Britain today (Al-Refai and Bagley, 2008). One of the paradoxes of pluralism is that in times of relative tolerance, barriers between the blocs of the plural society breakdown, or 'wither away' in a benign manner. This has certainly been the case in The Netherlands in which, in a climate of general secularism and welfare support for disadvantaged groups, the ideological basis of separate identities for Catholics, Protestants and humanists, between social classes, between ethnic groups from the Caribbean and Asia, and between parties of the extreme left and the extreme right has been eroded. This has resulted in an acceleration of the number of 'mixed marriages' in the Netherlands (Bagley, Van Huizen and Young, 1997). In Britain too, high rates of ethnic intermarriage illustrate that for some groups, the blocs or pillars of the plural society are dissolving.

Britain has for some decades been divided by those who hold markedly racist views (at least a fifth of the population), and those who strongly, and consciously reject racism, who number at least a third of the adult population. These progressive elements in British society are illustrated by the figures on mixed marriages (Platt, 2009). Platt found that nine percent of British children aged less than 16 could be described as "mixed race". These children reflected the fact that 48 percent of African Caribbean men and 34 percent of African Caribbean women who live in Britain, have a white, European partner. Children of these partnerships are thus counted as 'mixed race', and demographers estimate that because of this, within two generations African Caribbean as a racial group will have largely disappeared in Britain. Intermarriage rates for Indians in Britain are 11 percent; for Chinese, 35 percent; and for Pakistanis, four percent. But for racists, however much European ancestry a child has, he or she remains "black" even (as in apartheid South Africa) when only one grandparent was "black" or "coloured". Unless the separate blocs of a plural society remain rigidly apart through the political authority of a dominant group, within a police state (as in apartheid South Africa), there is a strong tendency for plural societies to change their character quite dramatically in the space of a few decades.

1.6 Poor or biased communications contribute to misunderstandings based on perceptions of culture, ethnicity and race

It is widely accepted that poor communications between individuals can create misunderstanding or misperception of an individual's culture, ethnicity and race, resulting in prejudice, stereotypes, victimisation, and even overt and covert racist practices. Historically for example, during the eighteenth century when Europeans began to explore Africa they thought that African people and their cultures were barbaric and ungodly. Thus there was the justification for slavery, and motives to Christianise African people. Early Europeans did not set out to learn about African cultures, their language, religions, cultural norms and expectations. Instead they categorised them as idle, treacherous, cruel, impudent, and dishonest. Ironically, those who were converted to Christianity remained slaves! And the many stereotypes held by Europeans about those whom they had enslaved tended to be self-confirming.

Today we still have a problem of accepting the true meaning of ethnicity and the contribution pride in ethnic heritage can make to society. Ethnicity is the social construct of a group or an individual within that group, based on shared or similar values, manners of social organisation, and assumed identity based on a shared lineage. (Hall 1992) expressed that the term *'ethnicity'* acknowledges the place of history, language and culture in the construction of subjectivity and identity, as well as the facts that all discourse is place, position, situated and all knowledge is contextual. Ethnic groups often share social, political, spiritual and cultural backgrounds, and for example they may speak the same language, worship God (or Gods) in the same manner, wear brightly designed costumes, and eat certain types of food. They usually form a minority group within a larger country population. For example in Britain, the indigenous population are in the majority of cases, of European origin, but within that national setting there are African Caribbean, Indians, Bangladeshis, Chinese, Somalis and many other ethnic minority groups.

In the United States, the majority of the population is of European ancestry too, but within or parallel to these ethnicities there are those who are Jewish, Hispanic, African American, Irish American, Puerto Rico, Mexican and many others. In both Britain and America (and in countries with migrant populations) not being able to communicate with the wider culture in their spoken mother tongue can lead to misunderstanding of their way of life, their belief systems, and social practices and norms.

1.7　Challenging racism in the health care workplace

Challenging racism in the workplace means than one needs to have a coherent philosophy of racism in the first instance. There is no simple explanation of racism, but there are common factors that are responsible for bringing it into existence, which include historical beliefs about racial superiority which are embedded within culture, currently prevailing norms about stereotyping, scapegoating, and describing 'negative' cultural differences. Racism is a belief system that advocates explicitly or implicitly, discriminating against people based on a perception of their supposed racial characteristics. Imposing racial characteristics on groups (e.g. calling all people with cultural origins in the Indian sub-continent as 'Pakis') provides a cognitive support for discriminatory practices. First comes racialised classification, then a set of beliefs and stereotypes about the group, and then a set of implicit or explicit behaviours which involve social avoidance, discriminatory actions, and even acts of violence. In addition, racist practices and behaviours are cultivated through socialisation in family groups and structures, schooling, teacher attitudes, peer groups and in institutional management and system.

It is also the belief of racists that each of the allegedly different races have different characteristics and aptitudes, which mean that they can be categorised as groups of superior and inferior intelligence, and with genetically programmed personality characteristics which make certain races predictable in their behaviour – some groups are stereotyped as violent, impulsive or mendacious for example (Coker 2001). Historically racism has thrived in virtually all civilisations, as a means of justifying exploitation, dominance, colonialism, slavery, and genocide. Thus Europeans enslaved people of colour based upon their ideology that Africans were inherently uncivilised; fit only for forced manual labour. In this ideology the dominant white race is superior and all other races are inferior.

It is vital that one needs to have comprehension of the history of racism, the types of racism and how residual racism can be practised in the organisations and environments in which we reside and work. The notion of racism starts with the belief that human beings can be grouped into different races, and certain races are inferior to others. There are different types of racism: for example there is institutional racism, which is a collective and organised system, maintained through overt and covert practices and policies that restrict opportunities for minority groups to develop to their full potential. In various social organisations and social systems which make up society, some white people maintain and sustain (consciously or unconsciously), a superior position with little or no opportunity for minority groups to be a part of decision-making power. Some minority members may have access to middle management and be able to contribute to the organisation in only a limited way. Institutional racism promotes and protects white and dominant group privilege through written and unwritten cultural rules. Many of these practices are cultivated in business organisations, hospitals, police forces, judicial and political systems, schools, colleges and universities, sport (especially at management levels), and in recreational centres, and in the performing arts.

1.8 Identifying examples of key strategies one can use to deal with racism

The development of self-confidence and self-awareness is one of the key strategies one has to use in order to comprehensively address covert or overt racism practices by individuals. According to Hick (2000) there are four main kinds of racism - historical, scientific, institutional, and 'new' racism. Recognition and comprehension of their definition is important, as well as an understanding of how they are used. This is critical for the psychological survival of a minority person in a racist environment. In addressing historical racism Hick (2000) shows that this form of racism focuses on lineage and common decent. This means that the person needs to be beware of, for example a group of people with common history that is not fixed by biological determinism - a group of people who share a common vision, mission, cultural aims and objectives, which help to live creatively and altruistically with different ethnic and cultural groups. Understanding the violent ideologies of the race-hatred industry serves as a foundation for self-development in the area of race and racial issues. It is important to know how some white-led organisations encourage hate-rage and violence expressed against groups of people (so called "racial groups") whom they considered to be inferior.

In modern society, individuals who are most likely to be highly prejudiced and to practise discrimination are those who have lower social status, poorer achievements in school and work, poorer self-esteem with neurotic traits, and those who suffer the syndrome of relative deprivation (Bagley et al., 1979; Bagley and Verma, 1979). These authors also point to culture as a factor in prejudice and discrimination – a whole nation may have inherited cultural traits disposing them to prejudice. Thus cross-cultural analysis, as Bagley and colleagues show, is a useful tool in understanding the dynamics of prejudice. They showed that the Netherlands, with a cultural history of tolerance, was a far less racist culture than Britain, whose colonial history disposed the average indigenous person towards intolerance of ethnic groups who had been oppressed or enslaved people of the colonies, before they (or their ancestors) emigrated to Britain.

In terms of social system variables, Bagley and Verma (1979) showed that older people, those who were poorly educated, and those with a sense of "status grievance", were the most prejudiced – typically sections of the white working class. Up to a third of the adult British population, according to various surveys between 1970 and 2008, hold prejudiced views about "race" and ethnicity, even though the targets of racist hostility are changing. Today African Caribbean are better tolerated, and it is Islamophobia, refugees and asylum seekers, as well as immigrants from Europe that are now the fetish of those who seek to foster racial hatred. On the positive side, at least a third of the indigenous 'white' population of Britain hold tolerant views about minorities, and it is this group (mainly younger, better educated, and in stable blue and white collar occupations) who are most likely to be in "mixed marriages" (Platt, 2009).

There is a vein of psychopathology in British racism, which is the province of those whose hatred of minorities is obsessive in nature, leading to the formation of groups of the far right, who engage in acts of violence against minorities. These groups draw their membership from the most depressed and violent of the white working classes. They lack formal social power, but their propensity for violence can make life very difficult for religious and ethnic minorities who have to live in areas of the city where these racist thugs want to prowl.

The person who is oppressed because of his or her colour should be knowledgeable of the person whom he or she is engaging with during social, cultural or political interactions. This means that one has to be aware of the white person's insecurities, anxieties, feelings and thought processes. The active racist's aim is to destroy, humiliate, segregate, isolate, stereotype, murderously attack, violate, and blame anyone that does not resemble them. These negative energies will have a profound effect upon the person of colour living in a shared environment. To be productive in negative surroundings, mean that the African Caribbean individual should have a deep sense of Afro-centric history and philosophy and be able to use this information as a motivational platform to be productive, entrepreneurial, intellectual, innovative, self-sufficient, resourceful, creative individuals. The same holds true for Asian and Islamic minorities. If we can strive for deep-rooted principles of equality and respect for life, and for one another, regardless of ethnicity, social class, religion, disability, gender or sexual orientation then we should be able to embrace the dignity of another human being irrespective of their race or colour.

Identifying a good mentor or role model is a significantly important tool that can be used for effective self-development. For example a mentor is someone you can trust and with whom you can develop a good relationship. A mentor will be an experienced person, for example in the field of race and ethnicity. A mentor can be your professional and personal friend or buddy who can help to provide assistance or support on how to deal with difficult situations in the work place, working towards a new career development and solving life challenges and crises. It should be someone whom you are able to communicate or interact with well and one who is willing to share with you his or her professional experiences. One can have more than one mentor, and you can also be a mentor for others – this will develop as you grow older, wiser, and more experienced! The important point is for one to have access to expert guidance, advice and support in ways that can help you to develop your true potential.

1.9　Strategies to be used to address institutional racism and racism in the work place

To address the concerns outlined above, the organisation needs to plan, formulate and implement strategies to promote equality, with diversity education training for all. This should be aimed at members of the organisation or institution who occupies strategic, operational and functional positions. Managers who have the responsibility for promoting and delivering diversity education, training and support should for example design programmes to increase awareness amongst staff on how to recognise their own privileges whilst working in the multicultural environment and the diverse workforce. Training programmes should include subjects such as ethnicity and victimology, forces of suppression and oppression, how to promote equality of opportunity within a white dominant control organisation to promote fairness, restore dignity, value and respect amongst all employees. These training programmes should be mandatory and should be made part of annual staff appraisals. Performance indicators should be used to evaluate and monitor how well the employers are supporting equality of practice, demonstrating accountability, responsibility, promoting harmony, productiveness and efficiency in the workforce. All hostile or negative incidents (based on hostility to someone because of their ethnicity, gender, religion, disability status, or sexual orientation) should be logged and presented every six months, with the aim of correcting negative institutional practices. These logs will include notes on hostility and discrimination by clients and patients towards members of staff as well

Raising ethnic, cultural and race awareness might be achieved through the collective celebration of an annual anti-racism week, in which the lives of great Britons, Caribbeans, Africans and Asians can be celebrated (for example, Florence Nightingale, Oscar Wilde, Bernard Shaw, Vera Brittain, William Wilberforce, Elizabeth Fry, Marcus Garvey, Martin Luther King, Mahatma Ghandi, and Dr. Ambedkhar, the Dalit leader). Workshops can address the issues of racial consciousness, anti-discriminatory practice, threatening behaviour, provocation to hatred, and how to identify and deal with racist propaganda, jokes and insults. Promotion of equality and diversity in the working environment should aim to promote a better comprehension of diverse work-force conflict, promoting insight into culture and organisational management, resolving group and individual differences, disputes, and conflict. This strategy is designed to encourage a better understanding of the cross-cultural issues and intercultural issues and seeks to improve inter-personal communication amongst staff.

Another strategy for employers is to try and create a balanced workforce by appointing ethnic minority staff, (as well as balancing gender appointments) at all levels within strategic, operational and functional areas. The organisation should make the effort to recruit black and ethnic minorities by placing advertisement in the ethnic new papers on radios, television and cable network services. It is vital that employers recognise the skills, knowledge, attitudes and productive habits that black and ethnic minorities can bring. A diverse workforce can provide the relevant skills information and be creative in ways that should increase levels of efficient and humane service within health care organisations because of their relevant cultural experience. Racism in the workplace stifles creativity and does not support free exchange of information of creative ideas. Racism, implicit or explicit, creates an environment for conflict, poor productivity and performance, and reduces the organisation's ability and effectiveness to be productive in the service, business and corporate environment. The aim of organisations ought to provide education and training that will encourage, develop and sustain meaningful relationships between colleagues, and hence improve work force performance in the health and social care service industry.

2.1   Strategies to promote multicultural health care in health care settings

First one needs to understand the concept of multiculturalism in order to offer appropriate health care in a diverse society. Within a multicultural society, there is diversity of languages, religion, cultural norms and expectations. Within this framework the manner in which individuals greet each other, communicate, and interpret information can have a profound impact on their relationships. For example, in the Islamic faith, when a person dies it is essential that the deceased is placed in a position where they face Mecca. Also it is important for the health professional to understand why only members of the Muslim faith are allowed to wash the deceased, and essential rituals must be performed by the Imam. Similarly, for the African Caribbean person who is a practicing Christian, it may be required that the local pastor should offer last rites which might (except for Calvinists) allow the patient to see forgiveness of their sins. The patient may also be baptised before dying. This act might ensure that the deceased's soul enters purgatory, paradise or heaven. In some African and Hindu religious rituals, it is believed that windows and doors should be left open to encourage the arrival of ancestors to help the deceased's journey to the spiritual world, or to enable the soul's rebirth as it moves from the now deceased body.

Most people of the Jewish faith (and especially Orthodox Jews) eat kosher food, which is slaughtered according to principles laid down in the Old Testament. Orthodox Jews are not allowed to eat pork or shellfish; and meat and milk cannot be eaten together. Each item needs to be placed into a separate container. For Muslims, meat must be slaughtered according to Halal principles, which are similar to Kosher methods. Like Jews, Muslims will not eat pork or shellfish, and also avoid alcohol. Jews, Muslims and Christians are "children of the book" - that is they share adherence to many rituals set out in the Old Testament. One group of Christians, Seventh Day Adventists, form a prominent church in the Caribbean Islands, and now provide a major source of worship centres for African Caribbean in the UK. Adventists adhere strictly to Old Testament dietary principles – no pork or shellfish, as well as avoidance of strong drinks which includes not only alcohol but also avoiding tea, coffee and cola drinks. Adventists keep the Sabbath Day (Saturday) holy, and like Orthodox Jews will do no labour, or undergo voluntary medical care between sunset on Friday until sunset on Saturday. Orthodox Sikhs will, for religious reasons, not eat Kosher or Halal food.

Most Rastafarians, a religious group with origins in Jamaica are vegetarians; even as meat-eaters they will abstain from pork, predatory fish, dairy products, white flour, and artificial sweeteners. They prefer to have natural juices made from fruits instead of artificial drinks such as soda and colas. They do not believe in eating tinned, sterilized or preserved food, which is seen as "dead food". Consuming such "dead food" amounts to treating the body as a cemetery. Adventists too require that its adherents treat "the body as a temple of the Holy Spirit" in diet, personal cleanliness, and self-presentation.

Based on the above examples, it is important that health care organisations respect the cultural practices and beliefs of the patient. This can be done, for example, by providing a multicultural menu that provides the patient with a wide choice of food. If this cannot be done, then management should engage collaboratively with local caterers to provide for the various minorities' ethnic needs. Providing multicultural health care means, for example, putting into place prayer rooms for Muslims to access, and also observing the right hand and left hand rule when bathing or feeding Muslim patients. Muslim rules regarding the privacy of female patients in relation to male health care personnel should be sympathetically followed. Health care information should be printed in various languages.

2.2 Diabetes and Cardiovascular Disease: Multicultural View Points

Information on personal health care should be made available to those who may be at special risk of certain health conditions. For example in Britain, diabetes, hypertension, heart attacks, strokes, obesity are found in quite a large percentage of the African Caribbean and Asian Community. Various studies suggest that Type 2 Diabetes (T2D) is up to three times as common in Britons of South Asian descent, and twice as common in Britons of African and African Caribbean origins, in comparison with European-lineage settlers to Britain. One may want to question why those diseases are dominant in both African Caribbean and Asian communities.

Comprehending the eating habit of both groups is important in order to provide the right advice and guidance in nutritional health care. For example, the diets of most African Caribbean contain predominantly carbohydrates. A typical eating pattern for African Caribbean is as follows. Breakfast may consist of ackee (tropical fruit) and salt fish; fried dumpling or fried bammy - boiled banana, cassava, or boiled yam; and hard dough bread. Tea may include cerassee tea, cocoa, milo, mint, rosemary and coffee. This is followed by lunch, which consists of patties made from beef, chicken, fish or mutton, bun and cheese, butter, corn bread and biscuits. Drinks are made from white or brown sugar with water called lemonade, pop or soda, and syrup. In the evening dinner consists of rice and peas; curried goat or chicken; jerk pork, fish or chicken; fried plantains or boiled banana, white or brown flour dumpling, yam, cocoa, breadfruit, cassava or bammy cakes.

Drinks are often made from carrot with ingredients such as condensed or evaporated milk, nutmeg, cinnamon, white or brown sugars sweetened to taste. Carbohydrates, fats and oils are the main nutritional ingredient in daily diets. This likely contributes to the high percentage of diabetes in their community. Providing a good eating plan for African Caribbean must be aligned with their cultural eating habits, together with an exercise programme for burning up excessive fat. Providing care means that healthy eating should be communicated to the group using a wide range of communication tools. Also, there should be emphasis made on the importance of eye and foot care, increasing knowledge about food and nutrition, heart diseases, kidney and nervous system problems, and possible medication. Increased knowledge should eventually change individual eating habits that may then reduce the risk of diabetes in this community.

Sharma and Cruickshank (2001), in a study of dietary and nutritional practices of a British African Caribbean population found that not all African Caribbean followed the same cultural customs regards diet. Those of Jamaican origin for example, had dietary customs that were different from those whose cultural origins were in Trinidad. Dietary customs survived across several generations of immigrants to Britain, although it is likely that in mixed marriages new cultural practices are being formed. The health professional must, therefore, be sensitive to the emerging cultural practices of their clients – a 'one size fits all' model should be avoided.

2.3 Should health diversity practices be embraced by healthcare professionals and organisations?

The concept of health diversity lies in the notion that health can be interpreted, diagnosed and communicated differently amongst various races of people. Several factors can contribute the health and well being of the individual. For example, nutrition, religion, language, social customs, belief and practices, family planning, festival, death, birth, marriage, abortion, donation of organs, post-mortem, funerals and dress codes; all have an impact on providing effective and professional care for a diverse population. Health is generally defined by the World Health Organisation (1946) as a state of complete, physical, mental and social wellbeing and not merely the absence of a disease or infirmity. Based on the above quotation, it is imperative that health personnel and institutions embrace all factors that can sustain good health in light of WHO's definition. When a nurse, doctor or professional cares for patients from ethnic minority background, it is vital that they do not impose their own values, beliefs, expectations and cultural practices on the care they are providing for people whose cultures differ from their own.

Most of the above beliefs concerning nutrition, religion, death, birth are cultural based - that is to say that are collectively placed within a unique framework of categories and subcategories, of shared belief systems and practices that have been woven in into the fabric of the community. Such belief systems and practices have been formulated and implemented over thousands of years, but change as time progress. These belief systems and practices influence people's life styles, patterns of thinking and expression, communication (either verbally or non-verbally), styles of behaviour, eating habits, and the interpretation of health, illness and diseases. Belief systems are part of a person's culture as Helman (1997) stressed in his book on health care. Cultural background has important influences on many aspects of a person's life, including perception, emotion, family structure, body image, attitude to pain, all of which may have implications for health care. For example, on the subject of food and nutrition, people may eat or abstain from certain types of food because of the beliefs people hold for these foods. For example, amongst some Ghanaians of West Africa, some may refuse to eat shell fish or water yams based on the belief that the products can bring misfortune and evil on the family.

African Caribbean, who are people of mainly Africans origins, found in the Greater and Lesser Antilles of the Caribbeans, Jamaica, Trinidad, Barbados, Antigua, Belize, Grenada, Dominica, St Lucia, Aruba, Bonaire, Curacao and Guyana; hold specific beliefs about different types of food and nutrition. In general many may avoid pork, meat, salt, spring chicken (tree frog), tea, coffee, food with preservatives and additives, snakes, dogs, cats and monkeys! Foods that are considered as a delicacy in one cultural group may be taboo in another culture. People may abstain from certain food types on the grounds that they are harmful to the body. For example, Rastafarians avoid salt, considered to be a taboo product, based on the biblical story regarding God turning the sinful woman into "a pillar of salt". Groups such as Jews, Muslims, Rastafarians and Seventh day Adventists abstain from pork, the eating of which is proscribed in the bible. Food such as butter (ghee) may be eaten by Hindus, Sikhs, Muslims and Jews. Both Jews and Muslims believe that animals need to be blessed and slaughtered in a special way - the food is then classified as Halal or Kosher. Some Sikhs, Buddhist and Hindus may eat chicken, goat and lamb. However, it should be noted that many followers of Buddhist and Hindu faiths do not eat animal products (including eggs) because of their appreciation and respect for life. Milk, yogurt and ghee are usually acceptable because no killing has taken place, and these foods are thought to promote harmony within the body, according to yoga principles. Sikhs (a monotheistic group who split from Hinduism) will not, for religious reasons, eat meet slaughtered according to Kosher or Halal rituals.

Many Jamaicans still believe in taking special formulated brewed drink made from herbs, fruit and vines to revitalise the body and to maintain good health. One product which immediately comes to mind is a "roots tonic wine" called Puteen, brewed and bottled by Samson's Herbal products in Clarendon, Jamaica, West Indies. Local produce includes nuts or seeds (usually peanuts), root of plants (usually coconut root, and chainey roots), plants (usually young banana shoots), herbs (usually ironweed, tuna, blood wiss, sarsaparilla) and other plant products which may be used to prepare this special tonic, marketed in Jamaica and imported to Britain as "Baba Roots". Saraspilla is widely used for arthritis, pains of the body, as a blood purifier, aphrodisiac, and for the treatment of scrofula diseases (controlled clinical trials of these claims are lacking!). It is, however, the prevalent belief amongst local inhabitants that this tonic increases sex drive, reduces impotence, and generally improves health status.

In the Chinese community, eating certain types of food is believed to have a significant effect on the balanced, physical element of the body. Traditional Chinese medicine believes that food is important in order to heat, cool and neutralise the body and to achieve a balance of one's health status (Southern Area Health Authority, Cultural Handbook for Staff, 2003.) It is believed that food groups help to maintain the harmony of *yin* and *yang* energy forces responsible for maintaining good health and for the sustenance of life. In addition, Chinese health stores (of which there are many in Britain) offer a range of herbal remedies dispensed by skilled practitioners, who will diagnose the appropriate remedy for any particular ailment and treatment (refer to www.aworldofchinesemedicine.com) for further information. Chinese culture too, is the originator of acupuncture (www.tcm.health-info.org), of which there are many practitioners in Britain. Acupuncture is widely used not only by Chinese people in Britain, but also by indigenous communities.

Similarly, Indian health practitioners offering ayurvedic medicine (based in principles of Hindu philosophy) are found in all major cities in Britain. This type of traditional medicine has similarities to

Chinese traditional medicine, in that it seeks to maintain a balance of bodily systems based on an understanding of "humours" of the body from an individual specific diagnosis (see www.ayurvedic-medicines.com). Yoga is also often taught by practitioners of traditional Indian medicine.

Belief systems grounded in a particular set of cultural values can have considerable impact upon individual health, beliefs and practices. For example in some African and African Caribbean cultures, for a person suffering from diabetes, and having a leg ulcer that has difficulty in healing, can sometimes lead to the cultural belief that the condition is caused by supernatural forces, or by someone who practices witchcraft, black magic or obeah. These beliefs, unfortunately, may hamper treatment models offered by NHS practitioners. There are some African-Caribbeans who believe that once one is over forty five, they will almost always develop diabetes. Beliefs about obeah may still be held by elderly patients of African-Caribbean origin, despite a considerable acculturation of traditional beliefs. There is no formal research on belief in obeah in British populations, since the trans-cultural psychiatric research of Kiev (1964). Amongst some African-Caribbean communities, individuals may consult the power of the local obeah man for health care and protection. Vassel (2006) commented on this in a poem in local Jamaican dialect, on the actions of a person who uses the Obeah man to impart a curse on anyone who interferes into his way of life

Trouble me and my obeah man
Will give you a sore foot
Then your goose will cook

Fast into my business and your tongue
Will become black like soot
No matter where you go
No doctor or nurse can heal it
De obeah will fix you good
Just like bag- o-wire on logwood
You better believe it
The foot will broke out into sore
Cause you to lame more and more
One piece of red cloth
You have to use for a bandage
People will know you foot belong
To my obeah man in marriage
Don't fast or interfere my business
Or you blood will turn into diseases
A ho- ho- ho (Vassel 2006)

The poem speaks about an individual who believed in the power of witchcraft, practised by a person capable of using his powers to curse an individual with a ulcer (sore foot), which cannot be healed by a health professional. The person who is cursed will have difficulties speaking because his/her tongue will be diseased and rotting (tongue black like soot). The sufferer will be forced to wear red bandage to protect the ulcer, which identifies to the public that he has been bewitched by an obeah man.

2.4   Conventional religion and beliefs about disease

For many, belief in God provides mental and psychological comfort, especially during times of suffering. However, in some cases when an individual has experienced great suffering they may think that God has abandoned them in their hour of need; this may result in mental health problems. Some, in the face of prolonged illness and disability, may experience spiritual, emotional, psychological, and cultural pain. The health professional needs to be aware that members of different ethnic groups, and particular faith groups, may experience and report their health-related problems in different ways.

Religious belief and ritual is a way of life for many in ethnic minority communities in Britain, and such beliefs and rituals often sustain the physical, psychological, spiritual health of the individual. Females of Hindu and Muslim faiths often prefer to be seen by female doctors, and consideration should be given to their desires for privacy and modesty when being prepared for operations, x-rays or gynaecological examinations.

Religions or faith groups such as, Islam, Christianity (including Protestants, Roman Catholics, Anglicans, Mormons, Christian Scientists, Seventh Day Adventists, Jehovah's Witnesses, Methodists, Quakers, Greek and Russian Orthodox adherents, and Maronites or Eastern Catholics), Hindus, Buddhists, Taoists, followers of Confucius and many others, may have specific beliefs and practices related to dress, diet, dying and death rites, bereavement rituals, burial or cremation customs, blood transfusions, post mortems, organ donations, marriage, birth, circumcision, child naming ceremonies, abortion and the right to life, as well as family planning. These factors have impact on the overall health and condition of individuals. Finally, embracing health diversity means that health care professionals should at all times treat the patient with respect, dignity, and should value the patient's opinion irrespective of their ethnic origin, religious, nutritional habits, colour or social class. The health professional should provide and offer appropriate health care, guidance, advice and education to patients irrespective of (but sensitive to) their cultural background or heritage, or health beliefs and practices. The prime aim for providers of health care is to work in collaboration and partnership with groups in the diversity of a multicultural environment.

2.5 Can understanding of cultural knowledge improve nursing practice in a multicultural society?

Understanding the concept of cultural knowledge is very important for the individual who has to administer care within a diverse or multicultural society. Thus Adams' (1995) interpretation of cultural knowledge is based on the context of familiarisation with selected cultural characteristics, history, values, belief systems and behaviour of members of different ethnic groups.

This knowledge provides opportunity for the health care professional with an appreciation of body language, dialect, special beliefs, and terms regarding health and illness. This approach may also help the carer to understand people's life styles and provides opportunity to deal with unfamiliar terminology during the communication process. Moreover, it can be used as a tool to improve, encourage and involve patients in their own health care. It enables the carer to show empathy and solidarity when addressing individual and group-related illness, as well as being open-minded, flexible and tolerant when dealing with diverse health issues. Health organisations and professionals must be aware of the effect inadequate cultural knowledge can have on the health care of individuals from different racial and cultural disparities.

The *Diabetes UK* report 2004 documented that South Asian population with diabetes consist of the following: Indian-origin, 89,000 known cases; Pakistani-origin, 42,000; and Bangladeshi-origin, 12,000 - totalling 143,000. The report noted figures for Black African and Caribbean populations with diabetes as follows: Black Caribbean, 60,000; Black African, 36,000; and other Black populations in UK, 3,000 - a total of some 99,000 individuals. Ethnic minority people with these illnesses are particularly likely to live in the British Midlands, and therefore, local health care professionals must be fully aware of the social, medical and cultural needs of these minorities. In the case of African-Caribbean and diabetes, health practitioners should have firm grasp of cultural knowledge on traditional diets and foods, if they are to successfully engage in dialogue and offer treatment on how to deal with this disease. Preparing certain foods, serving and eating food within family and other groups often plays a vital role in culture and identity of people in many different ethnic groups. This argument is same for Asians groups, who often adhere to a particular diet because of its cultural significance. Knowledge of these dietary practices and rituals will help the Nurse or Doctor to plan diet with patient, in order to control the disease without being disrespectful of the patient's cultural beliefs. For example, during the month of Ramadan Muslims will fast for the whole day, but may break their fast with high calorie foods which are high in sugar and carbohydrates. Any dietary programme has to incorporate these challenges.

2.6 Importance of intercultural communication in the health care environment

- To provide good service that respects all belief and values of patient.
- To understand how patients use local dialects and phrases to explain their health problems.
- To build trust between patients and nurses.
- To understand the patient's belief about a particular disease.
- To know more about a patient's culture, religion, and their way of life.
- To enable nurses to interact with patients comfortably, and reduce errors of misinterpretation during the

communication process.

- Help patients to build trust and confidence with the nurse and to also understand patient's needs and wants and expectations of health care.
- To build trust and respect between carers, patients and the families.
- To understand a patient's background which will help provide a better service.
- To treat the patient as an individual and not to generalise.
- To make patients aware of their illness, treatment and to avoid conflict with patients and their families.
- To ensure that nurses do not feel intimidated when conversing with patients who are describing their illness in their cultural perspective.
- To understand a patient body language because in each person's culture, body language can mean different things to individuals from different cultures or ethnicities.
- To understand how patient thinks and behave when they are experiencing illness.
- To show cultural empathy in the time of bereavement and personal grieving.
- To provide a holistic care for patient on request.
- To avoid using words that may cause distress to patient.
- To ensure that patients understand the treatment they are receiving for their illness, and to ensure that the patient makes informed choices.
- To provide health care information accessible to the cultural understanding of

the patient.
- To learn more from patient about the types of herbs and plants they use to treat diseases and ailments
- To give individuals the feeling of belonging and acceptance whilst they are being cared for in hospital. To break down cultural barriers that can affect health care practice, for example, countering ethnocentrism.
- To avoid and prevent being prejudiced, racist, sexist or stereotyping of individual patients.
- To understand why some patients are themselves hostile or racist in their beliefs and attitudes, especially when their carers come from ethnic minority groups.
- To understand the reasons why Asians find English meals (and hospital food especially) bland, tasteless or lacking in flavour.
- To accurately explain the nature of the illness to patient without causing offence or misunderstanding.
- Getting the patient to understand and take responsibility for their well being.
- How to listen to patients and their families and how to show respect to elders.
- How to understand how individuals of different cultures respond to pain.
- To help the patient express their feeling about their illness without feeling insecure or invaluable.
- To ensure that cultural difference are recognised, and empathy and trust are maintained.

2.7 How can nurses improve cross-cultural communication with patients?

> ➤ Use qualified interpreters.
> ➤ Use pictures or photographs, health plays, and traditional tales and poems to explain health and illness.
> ➤ Learning some words or phrases from the languages of ethnic groups with whom you are frequently in contact; or have a translation book handy.
> ➤ Learning more about different types of cultures and their boundaries.
> ➤ By asking patient and families, if possible, about their experiences of health care in another country.
> ➤ By attending cultural awareness training day and seminars.
> ➤ By networking with different ethnic minority groups on health care projects.
> ➤ By being more polite, for example how to say good morning or greeting the patient.
> ➤ Learning how to interpret non-verbal communication across cultures.
> ➤ By speaking to patient and families from different cultural backgrounds.
> ➤ To research and write article on cultural health care issues.
> ➤ Spending more time with patient and getting to know the patient.
> ➤ In their break or tea time they could watch cultural health care programmes.
> ➤ By attending basic language workshop for example how to say *"Good morning"* in

Welsh, Spanish, Punjabi, Urdu, Polish, Hindi, Jamaican and others languages or dialects.

➢ Leaning about a patient's belief, religion, spirituality, food, gender, and gender privacy issues.

➢ To be actively involved in evidence-based research to promote cultural health care practices.

➢ Listen more effectively to the patient and let them feel valued.

➢ By reflecting on previous encounters with patients.

➢ Assessing at all tine on how the cultural communication can be improved.

➢ By attending cultural festivals, birth and marriage ceremonies, places of worship to learn and interacting with people from different cultures.

➢ Asking the patient frequently if they understand what was being said to them about their illness or disease.

➢ Asking general question about culture before personalising questions about individual culture and belief systems.

➢ Understand how eye contact, facial expression, and touching can be either offensive or respectful in different cultures.

➢ Learn proper forms of address, especially for older patients; don't automatically use "Christian names".

➢ Understand why the patient may believe in supernatural spirits or forces, which may enable nurse to appreciate the belief system of the patient, for example on how spirituality is used to comfort the sick and dying.

➤ To interact more with the patient's family, and learn how the family manages illness according to their cultural traditions. To ensure that nurses who are inexperienced in dealing ethnic minority health care issues are matched with mentors to provide counselling and guidance.

➤ Know how to communicate with the elderly sick patient, from African, Afro-Caribbean and Asian cultures.

➤ Celebrating culture and diversity events in the caring environment.

➤ Ensure that staffs are culturally competent, sensitive and knowledgeable as they execute their daily health care practices in the caring environment.

➤ Seek information directly from the patient through interaction, and asking them questions.

➤ During the cultural conversation, talk about yourself and then encourage the patient to reciprocate in the process.

3.1 Examples of how some patients describe their illnesses or disease to health care professionals?

Illness or Diseases	Examples Cultural expressions / country / source
Angina	Got a dickey rocker
Asthma	Tight throat (Hardie et al., 2000) Itchy throat Hurt to breathe Shortness of breath Wheezing Ribs illness – (Congo) Is my chest Chest feel tight
Bladder problem	Water works
Broken bones	Boo Bruk hand Brock bone (Jamaica)
Cancer	Growth (Jamaica) Tumour (Jamaica) Agassi (Virulent weed) Greek Cypriot – (Papadopoulos & Lees, 2004) Kakos (Badness) Greek Cypriot –

	(Papadopoulos & Lees, 2004) Sashimi acrostic (Ugly illness) Greek Cypriot (Papadopoulos & Lees, 2004) Famous (Black death) Greek Cypriot (Papadopoulos & Lees, 2004) Bernoulli (Bubonic fever) Greek Cypriot (Papadopoulos & Lees , 2004) Mari acrostic (Black illness) Greek Cypriot (Papadopoulos & Lees , 2004) Nar (Ulcer, sore) Bangladeshi (Papadopoulos & Lees, 2004)
Diabetes	Sweet blood Sweet water Sweet urine Sugar Thirst I can't quench Scary disease – USA (Taylor, 2004) Having two sugars Can't stop shaking Funny head sensation
Diarrhoea	Go the runs Bad belly Watery stool Runny stool Loose gut Defecating through the eye of needle Tummy tits Got the dolly mitts Loose bowel

	Hot illness (Haiti)
Erectile dysfunction	Can't get up Can't stand up Dead
Head aches	Knocks in the head (Zimbabwe) In pain Blinding headache
Gonorrhoea	Clap Burnt head Hot urine (France) Goon Bomb
Gynaecological	Problem down stairs Women problems Problem with water works
Haemophilia	Thin blood
Heart attack	A stabbing pain in the centre of his chest Diffuse pain in her neck and arm Tight chest Heavy chest Shooting pain Heart burn Heart ache
Heart burn	Bemuses Indigestion
Heart palpitation	Heart beating fast
HIV/AID	Best before (Zimbabwe) The virus Acid blood

Hypertension	Heavy head High blood pressure BP Pressure
Impotence	Can't get it up Can't stand Weak back Firing blanks
Jaundice	Yellow skin I am yellow
Learning disability	Screaming, noisy Retard
Loss of sensation in feet	Pins and needles Numb foot
Mental health	Loose screw Bonkers Go mad Flip one wig Looney Stark raving mad Out of my mind Losing wits Lose marbles Weak mind Senselessness Mess up me head
Migraine	Light hurts Dot in the eyes Eyes feel bruise Piercing head aches
Piles	Had a visit from farmer Giles

Schizophrenia	Hearing voices Voices in my head Seeing things Affected by the devils Conversation in my head
Tonsillitis	Sore throat neck
Tuberculosis	Ribs illness (Congo) Blood cough
Urethral infection	Burning pipe
Vomiting	Throwing up
Water retention	Swollen legs
Stroke	Severe hiccups, facial pain and nausea

3.2 Reflections on Multiculturalism in Nurse Educator Settings

One of the key strategies for strengthening Adult Education is the implementation of fundamental principles that promote the concept of Cultural Diversity in the teaching and learning environment, from a nurse education viewpoint. This environment can be one of the most culturally diverse, interactive and sensitive surroundings that enhance the academic and educational development of student nurses. Tutors need to comprehend the various interacting forces such as social, political, anthropological and technological issues, which will have an impact on the learning rate and achievement of students. This phenomenon is grounded on the hypothesis and principle that students come from different backgrounds, share different ideologies, beliefs, practices, norms and habits. These factors are inherited from socio-cultural and environmental perspectives, and are part of the lived experiences in the teaching and learning environment. Verma and Ashworth (1986) reminded us that those individuals, whatever their cultural backgrounds are not merely cultural beings but also social beings, as these facets of being human are inseparable. Within a diverse education forum, students will display a variety of behavioural qualities and it is the teacher's responsibility to harmonise these distinctive characteristics, so that students work together as a single unit while achieving their desired outcomes.

The word 'diversity' can mean different things to each individual in their respective places. Coker (2001) explained that diversity comprises of both visible and non-visible differences, which include religion, ethnicity and age. In matters of nurse education and health care, Campinha-Bacote (2003), argued that transforming demographics and economies influence our emerging multicultural work, and the inequality issues in the health status of people from different cultural backgrounds have challenged health care providers and organisations to consider cultural diversity as priority. Consequently, acknowledging and celebrating diversity can promote the respect of people's rights, endorses social justice, embraces differences in people and their conditions, recognises and acknowledges the complexity of their personalities, and the nature of their distinctiveness.

Each cultural group has its own unique knowledge, beliefs, values, practices, traditions and customs that make them exceptional in their wider community. Hindus, Sikhs, Jews, Rastafarians, Christians, and other religious and spiritual groups have within their structural framework various symbols, rituals, language constructs, folkways, ethical and moral values that are responsible for creating and maintaining their self-identity and their cultural image in the wider community. Within these organisations, a range of diverse identities do of course exist, such as sexual orientation, personal life styles, gender and gender orientation, physical challenges, language and paralanguage, communication styles within the group and in their relationships with other community groups. For example, awareness of a particular culture such as those in Hindu or Muslim ethnic groups can provide a useful short cut to understanding the general beliefs, values and behaviour of an individual, but there is a possibility that the individual can be stereotyped as a result of differences. Sanders and Ewart (2005) suggest that whatever their cultural or ethnic background, no two individuals are the same, and each should be treated uniquely. For these important reasons, the dynamism of cultural diversity creates a challenge for academics, professionals, business organisations, educators and educational establishments – the challenge of including and addressing a wide of range issues. These range from social, political, spiritual, psychological, class, ethnicity and religion, any disability, their gender orientation, family status, age, ancestry, language, place of residence, socioeconomic background, gender, as well as equality and inequality concerns that students bring to the teaching and learning environment. These factors may have a significant impact on the performances and accomplishments of students as they strive to attain their educational aspirations within the environments of schools, colleges, universities, and professional education centres.

From the viewpoint of nurse education, the classroom is one of the most potent arenas that can be used by educators to both instruct and bring together students from different ethnic backgrounds, irrespective of their colour, religious affiliation, belief and value systems, caste or class. This can lead to the sharing of knowledge, skills and good practice that can influence the learning and teaching of a specific curriculum. Through academic dialogues, cultural and sensitive issues such as HIV/AIDS, tuberculosis, impotence, hypertension, diabetes, health myths and other concerns, which might affect the health of a population, can be debated with spirit and zest.

The final goal is that of improving and providing efficient and effective care for the sick, and for the dying. In this way, the vibrant forces of diversity have the potential to bring people together, to share their varied experiences, challenge the status quo, re-write structured curriculum to address their individual needs, wants and expectations of the community, innovate new ways of teaching and learning for all, and use the potentially erudite information elicited to strategically plan for the future health care of the nation.

Since the teaching and learning environment is the propelling mechanism for creating a sense of achievement, excellence, recognition and positive image in students, the ideology of diversity challenges the teacher to embrace its value and meaning in the classroom. It sculptures of the individual, as well as a way forward for continued growth and value of the institution, both locally and nationally by encouraging curriculum designers to provide an education system that is inclusive, non-discriminatory and one which promotes interracial, cultural respect for learning. A diverse student population can persuade teachers to recognise that learners come from different backgrounds, and may learn and achieve at different rates, sometimes using contrasted cognitive styles (Bagley and Mallick, 1998).

Teachers understanding these important matters

will allow for flexible learning and teaching styles, including the innovation of teaching approaches with the potential to disseminate new knowledge and good habits in various subject areas. For example, the student nurse brings into the learning environment solid health and illness information which, when shared, can give a useful insight as to the reasons why the community or individuals hold certain beliefs about a particular disease, which may be helpful or perhaps hinder how the sickness can be optimally and holistically treated.

The health practitioner's aim should be to balance 'rational' treatments with the patient's understanding of his or her illness, its causes and traditional cures according to particular cultural beliefs, and the total cultural matrix within which health care, combining rational and humane treatments, can be delivered. It is important to remember that after discharge from clinic or hospital, the patient will return to a cultural milieu which sees the illness in ways which are often different from those of 'modern' medicine.

Capturing such vital health information can only be possible if the concept of cultural diversity is implemented in the institution, that permit teachers to ensure that all student needs are catered for in a diverse learning setting. Techniques such as differentiation and teaching with emotional intelligence are key tools that can be used by teachers to enhance the learning position of learners. Both techniques when effectively applied can provide and encourage the students to be independent, and to gain more control over their learning and the pace at which they set to achieve their lifelong learning goals.

To make learning and teaching more successful, the concept of differentiation has become a well-established ideology following the 1988 Education Act in the United Kingdom. The significance of this notion has been embraced by educational institutions, with the interpretation and inspiration that tutors should consider how they could provide effective and valuable teaching methods, for a diverse student population with diverse abilities and aspirations. It is necessary to address this because of the range of interests and motivations that make up the class. This educational model aims to ensure that all students have the opportunity to achieve their full potential, gain new skills, knowledge and goals, that will enable the individual to contribute in effective ways to health care institutions. Embracing the concept of differentiation, verifies the point that important issues, such as learning styles amongst students are important factors for educators to consider when designing tasks and group activities to aid the learning process.

The teacher's position, in a diverse teaching environment, must take into consideration factors such as the group ability, devoting additional time to students with learning needs, providing different levels of support material, and accepting the different levels and modes of presentation by students. In addition Vassel, (2006) suggests that differentiation encourages lecturers to revisit key principles of the learning process, and not to assume that the application of a general teaching strategy is the right approach for all students. In this case, the role that cultural diversity plays offers lecturers the opportunity of practising and encouraging inclusive learning styles for a diverse group of students. From this angle, individual learning programmes, sharing information, trust, confidence, commitment, and cooperation will be the fundamental elements that will encourage good and productive tutor-student relationships.

The vitality of cultural diversity creates opportunities for teachers to embrace the concept of "emotional intelligence" teaching and learning in the environment. Salvoey and Mayer (1990) define emotional intelligence as the subset of social intelligence that involves the ability to monitor one's own and others' feelings and emotions, to discriminate amongst them, and to use this information to guide one's thinking and actions. At this juncture, teaching with emotional intelligence requires the teacher to manage his or her own emotions, to be self aware and able to motivate oneself, and also to have the ability to show empathy and demonstrate the capability to handle relationships in both positive and creative ways. In the first instance, teachers should be able to recognise the factors that are responsible for changing emotions affecting self-concept as a learner, for instance from a feeling of enthusiasm to a feeling of anxiety. Such recognition should enable the teacher to identify what has caused negative feelings, and to examine how those feelings may affect his or her performance in the teaching and learning situation.

The ability to self assess one's feeling should allow the tutor to identify strengths and weaknesses of their emotions, reflect and implement appropriate strategies to correct negative emotions which could interfere with interaction and instruction. By doing this, the teacher will be able to present themselves with self confidence, highly motivated, self assured and with a positive presence in the class room situation. Founded on the above premises, should any interpersonal conflict arise between tutor and student, one should be able to manage the problem professionally, maintain classroom discipline and effective relationship between the class members and the teacher. Empathy provides the opportunity for the tutors to relate to their feelings and concerns with mixed student populations, while simultaneously appreciating the differences on how students express their feelings about things.

The teacher should be able to examine these feelings when expressed, value the unique thoughts of students and help them to develop strategies to cope, so that their achievement and performance on programmes will not be affected. From this perspective the teacher should be able to display social, intellectual and psychological skills. Also they can demonstrate leadership skills, as noted by Ashforth and Humphrey (1995); attain group performance goals; and improve individual performance, as acknowledged by Goleman (1995), in the teaching and learning environment. This ultimately can result in teachers and students caring about each other's feelings, showing sensitivity and comprehension of each other's perspective. Furthermore, the lecturer is encouraged to seek ways of meeting the needs, wants and expectation of the learners. Sensitive issues such as racism, prejudice, stereotyping and gender preferences can be dealt with transparently, competently and enable the lecturer's vision of diversity, as a window of opportunity for creating positive teaching and learning, where various students can work in harmony, be accountable and responsible for personal performance in the institution. On the other hand, to be unaware of one's emotion can affect how lecturers relate to students during in the classroom settings. Negative emotions in tutors can result in blaming students for the feelings of confusion or self-doubt that they may be experiencing. This can lead to embarrassment and stress in teachers and students.

Furthermore, lack of intercultural knowledge, or cultural 'blindness' can act as a catalyst for unfriendliness, un-cooperativeness and can create barriers that prevent the nurturing of good communication networks, sharing information to aid the learning and the teaching process of a student. The teacher needs to remain relaxed and collective, so as to create a positive learning environment, free from fear and psychological manipulation, when dealing with mixed student groups. Moreover, diversity understanding encourages the implementation of learning support strategy for students. In addition, it motivates students to be proactive by taking the responsibility to plan assignment deadlines, and to seek guidance and counselling on academic matters that are of particular concern. This enables tutors to play a more direct role in the educational development and achievement of the student, and to be aware of any personal problems that hinder the student's ability to learn and communicate on academic or personal issues. In this model of diversity, direct respect for all excludes the possibility of marginalisation amongst students. Marginalisation in the classroom encourages inequality practices such as prejudice, stereotypes, labelling, discrimination, segregation, undervaluing, restriction of learning information, denial of group independence, and reduction of opportunities for students to take the lead role in their learning and development. As a consequence, diversity in the teaching and learning environment has the potential for promoting cooperation amongst students, teacher and the teaching community on the whole.

Additionally the principles of diversity encourage the development of partnerships between community groups and the educational institutions, by providing an interface where all participants can enter into collaborative arrangements. For example, to identify financial resources for acquiring buildings to develop and maintain health education projects vital to the community. Diversity welcomes the strategy for expansion and diversification of extended community curricular programmes, and should enable each partner to be accountable and responsible for partnership events. In addition, human resources provided by both types of collaborator (students and teachers) are fundamental for sharing good skills, knowledge and positive practices in maintaining and sustaining fruitful partnership ventures.

The exclusion or marginalisation of people from different social, religious, class and cultural backgrounds, as well as different ability needs from mainstream education, cannot be tolerated in a diversity-based educational system. Teachers, who are reluctant to embrace transparency of diversity, should be offered the opportunity to be retrained and be prepared to take on the challenges that the phenomena propose. Embracing cultural diversity motivates teachers to welcome inclusiveness as an essential and effective tool, which can be used to counter internal conflicts amongst students, and can also produce reliable, productive and skilled persons as well as building stable and co-operative communities.

One of the key areas that are influenced by diversity is of language and communication. The language used in teaching has it economic value in the education world. It is ideally responsible for the socially upward progress of students. However, in a diverse learning environment Thompson (2003) advises that intercultural communication is prospectively a minefield of difficulty, and complication at both a theoretical and a practical level. This is because no one can communicate without being a part of the broader culture, and culture is a complex and multifaceted entity. Diversity allows the teacher to reflect on the language styles and usage during interaction with students. Synchronisation of the communication effort between teachers and students must be maintained in order to prevent misunderstanding of different language usages. Thompson (2003) further affirmed that the use of the spoken word, combined with paralanguage and body language, can produce a set of complex dynamics in all teaching and learning circumstances.

Based on the above reasoning, tolerance of diversity should ensure that teachers will have knowledge of the way students communicate in multicultural settings, as well as knowledge of the meaning and use of facial expressions, eye contact when speaking, posture, speed, tone and rhythm, and dress code. All of this needs to be understood in order to make certain that meaningful communication takes place and, at the school level, can help to reduce absenteeism, truancy, under-performance and dissatisfaction amongst students. It also focuses on promoting positive values, and importantly can facilitate the teaching style remarked on by Fiske (1990), which recognises that this type of culturally-inclusive communication helps to say something about our identity, and outlines a sense of who were are.

From this viewpoint, tutors need to ensure that the basic concept of the communication process, both verbally and written, is understood and maintained, to guarantee that vital information is passed on to aid the teaching and learning process in diverse classroom settings. This is very important from a nursing education standpoint, as these practices provide the pathway for the nurse to emulate good practice while in training, with the opportunity to transfer these principles to practice in their professional spheres. For example, nurse's failure to consider a patient's diversity, language needs and cultural underpinning can even lead to misdiagnosis of health-related problems, the dispensing of inappropriate medication, the development of mistrust between the patient and the nurse. The consequence of these concerns could eventually lead to poor application of nurse care.

Cultural diversity in the educational field enables tutors to recognise and implement equal opportunities for all learners. Each pupil brings to the school unique knowledge, skills and attitudes by interacting with parents and peers, throughout their everyday experiences of the world and the media. In addition, Vassel (2004) asserts that when diversity is recognised and identified in the institution, it guarantees that educators not only plan effectively for curriculum delivery, but also encourages tutors to take into account differences in student expectations, knowledge and experiences, and therefore, make sure the programme is interesting, relevant and appropriate in content. The outcomes of this, within the education process, should see the learning of specific skills and the imparting of knowledge aimed at the specific learning rate of an individual student. The philosophy of cultural diversity encourages the need to show respect, tolerance and appreciation for each other. It can discourage gender stereotyping and can address issues relating to the under-representation of ethnic minority staff in colleges and universities. It guarantees that opportunities are created for staff development and training for all teachers, in all subject areas pertaining to diversity and the teaching and learning environment. Settings of cultural diversity can help to mould positive attitudes in pupils and in older students toward their studies, and may with support and guidance, launch the individual towards creating learning to be good role models or mentors in the community, and in areas of employment. The role that cultural diversity plays, in educational establishments, is that of ensuring lecturers and other educators are culturally competent in the classroom environment. Campinha-Bacote (1999) writes that to be culturally competent, one should strive continuously to achieve the ability and availability, to effectively work within the cultural context of a client. Hence, working toward cultural competence, according to Campinha–Bacote requires one to self examine the degree of one's cultural awareness, cultural knowledge, cultural desire and cultural skills. Teachers and lecturers need to have the cultural desire to want to be engaged in a teaching and learning environment that accommodates a wide background of students. This author further argues that cultural desire motivates the individual towards the process of being culturally aware, culturally knowledgeable, culturally skilful and seeking cultural encounters (Campinha-Bacote 1999).

Based on the above theories, the politics of cultural diversity in the teaching and learning environment challenges teachers to examine their own attitude towards students from various ethnic representations. This is important because teachers, who are culturally incompetent or culturally insensitive, can send wrong signals to students. For example, teachers using language when it is not gender neutral can be interpreted and perceived as being biased; likewise, language use may betray prejudice or racist attitudes because of a student's physical attributes, mental attributes, gender orientation, ethnicity, caste or race. Typecasting of students can result in the non-participation of the students in academic debates, and the loss of opportunity to discuss and share important information, that could be of educational benefit to the class and the tutor. Ideally, diversity should empower students to challenge unfair practices or to question inequality practices. Teachers need to be aware that every student is different, and enters into the classroom with individual behaviour patterns and learning styles, and should lead by example with practices that promotes individual learning, rather than practices that encourage or have the potential to support conflict, disrespect and distrust. It is imperative that teachers create an environment of trust and reciprocal respect, so as to gain a transparent understanding of culturally diverse issues that could hinder achievement. In addition, they should devise strategies that will enhance quality development in learners. The student needs to experience teachers treating them as individuals, rather than as ciphers or simply as members of a group, or members of a caste, race or gender set. As the poem by Vassel (2006) relates, there are vital reasons why a student should be treated as an individual, giving the tutor an opportunity to foster productive partnerships:

Talk about cultural diversity
Does it provoke curiosity?
Should it encouraged inclusiveness
I have my own language you see and hear
I speak Hindi, Punjabi Spanish, Jamiekan and Urdu,
Without intimidation or fear
I have my own culture, spirituality my religion,
My Nubian Gods and my myths and my nutrition
See I am vegetarian not omnivorian.
I have my own history of ancient times
Written in western pages variously.
See you I am different in my roots and identity
But we can work together to participate and collaborate
On things that matters to you and me and them.
You and I don't have to waste the faith,
Together we can make contribution

*To make life better for our society, our community
at large.*
*Do away with insanity and false piety, that is
madness.*
*Start with respect and value our ancestors our
tutors and peers indeed*
*Attempts to disregard my feeling only brings grief
undesirably.*
Lack of admiration bring confusion and rebellion.
*Cultural diversity promotes cohesion and solution
to problems*
*Like underachievement, illiteracy, truancy, health
and obeah,*
*Come it's time to sit and reason in true friendship
season.*
*Come let us make a difference for all to see far and
wide*
*Come let start by taking positive action – start to
act*
Let's forget all negative act.
Start in a room that is culturally saturated
*With good skills, knowledge and positive attitude
it takes,*
*When equal opportunity practice is transparent
and in place to*
Prosper cultural richness, for a change.
(Vassel 2006)

The above ode transparently captures the
thoughts and feelings of an individual, who is
concerned about the acceptance of his cultural
heritage by another person. The argument
presented in the poem suggested that individual
cultures often have a unique set of cultural beliefs
and values that should be respected. An invitation
is offered that persuades the person to consider
the real opportunities to be gained, if a meaningful

collaboration and partnership that could be beneficial to society and to themselves is engaged in. Of course, expecting that one's cultural beliefs and practices should be accepted is a co-operative process: each cultural group should tolerate and accept the world view of other cultural groups; and within the pluralistic state, all cultural groups should respect the law which protects others, as well as expecting the state to protect them against arbitrary actions, such as racial and ethnic discrimination, racially aggravated attacks, and denial of freedom to worship and wear symbols of religious dress and identity.

In conclusion, the discussion in this section gives an indication of how dynamic diversity can be in the teaching and learning environment. Its variables provide both teachers and educational institutions with the chance to strategically plan, implement, evaluate and effectively provide resources to meet the needs, wants and expectation of students from a diverse background in a controlled environment. This requires understanding, unceasing and persistent effort if the organisation is to be successful in these endeavours. The learning network comprises of individuals with different communication patterns, interpersonal interaction styles, and a variety of values that need to be understood by the tutor. Through effective communication in the classroom, students can be exposed to a wide range of issues that can be examined, thereby challenging existing perspectives while simultaneously developing the student's critical, analytical and problem solving skills. From the teacher's standpoint it enables the tutor to gain a greater understanding of student values and differences, and also a chance for the teacher to promote good student and staff communications and relationships and how to function cooperatively in a diverse educational environment. Differences in age, gender, ethnicity, language background, ability/disability and socio-economic status require flexible approaches to teaching and learning that are supportive of the diversity of backgrounds, abilities and interests represented in the student population (UWA, 1997).

Cultural diversity creates a caring environment that accommodates and prepares students for the job environment, where they will have opportunities to engage with a diverse work force in various business and health care settings. Hence, diversity is a key tool that can be used to harness and develop latent skills, geared towards the improvement and productivity of people and organisation in a multicultural society.

3.3   Why should health care professionals be aware of a patient's religion?

Religion plays a vital role in representing the faith and worship of a patient. It is used as a vehicle to express the patient's belief and cultural behavioural practice of a particular conviction. In time of illness, sickness or bereavement, a person's religious faith provides the platform for assurance, expectation of divine healing and a pathway to communicate with God, for example through prayer, song, medication, or fasting. In providing care, a person's religion sets the framework for the medical and social care to be offered. It is important that the care plan, which is designed for the patient, does not interfere with the religious philosophy of the individual.

Many religious practices of a patient contribute towards bringing the individual closer to 'God'. The concept of God, from an Islamic belief setting, is one which means to a Muslim that Allah is the Almighty Creator and Sustainer of the universe, who is similar to nothing, and nothing can be compared to Him. The Western concept of God amongst some believers is that God is unlimited with regards to knowledge (omniscient), power (omnipotence), extension (omnipresence), and moral perfection; and is the creator and sustainers of the universe. Some members of the Christian religion believe that God is a father and through the Holy Spirit, personal bonding can be made with God. The Sikh perceives 'God' as being immortal, representing the eternal truth, one who is without fear, not constrained by time and is beyond death and birth.

When a patient experiences illness or poor health, the practice of religion often draws the patient nearer to God, in spirit or by faith. It is vital that the religious and spiritual belief of the patient is respected in order to provide a sensitive and caring service. Research carried out by Kuyvenhoven et. al. (1999) amongst Dutch General Practitioners on whether doctors paid attention to the religious beliefs of their patients, revealed that 'limited attention is paid to patients' religious beliefs and attitudes in routine daily work in general practice - most GPs do not register the religion of the patient'. In addition, 'Religious motives become increasingly important in the management of major life events such as abortion, terminal illness or euthanasia'. Likely, the same is true of British health practitioners.

In the United Kingdom an investigation done by Enoch et al (2003), sought the views of religious leaders (UK) on whether 'Informed consent should be obtained from patients to use products (skin substitutes derived from placenta) and dressings containing biological material.' The Catholic Bishops' Joint Bio-Ethics Committee felt that consent is necessary in the use of human skin. Also the Chairman of the Hospital Liaison Committee for Jehovah's Witness (Liverpool, UK), mentioned that each person must conscientiously make their own individual choice, made on after full information had been given to the patient. Leaders of the Muslim religion (Official Islamic Institute of Fatwa, Cairo, Egypt) agreed with the usage of all biological products except those obtained from pigs. Furthermore, the leader of the Chinese Multicultural Society (Birkenhead, Merseyside, UK) reported that among their members, products obtained from cows are unacceptable to all Hindus and some Buddhists, The Canon of the Anglican Church (Chester, UK) opined that any product derived from foetal material should not be used in medical treatments. To provide an effect and professional care, the awareness of religion in a patient's life is paramount, as it will ensure health professionals can work more effectively with a diverse population people from a variety of ethnic and religious back grounds.

Hawkins and Allen (1991) in The Oxford Encyclopaedia English Dictionary define religion *'as the belief in superhuman controlling power* esp. *in a personal God or gods entitled to obedience and worship.'* Each religion has a unique expression of worship and faith systems that bind worshippers to together. Religion has frameworks of ethics, morals, values, beliefs, attitudes and practices governed by a person or institutions that uphold its principles through commitment, devotion and faith. There are different types of 'religion' - for examples Humanism, which usually consist of adherents who do not believe in the existences of supernatural forces, God or Gods. Christianity is considered to be the world's biggest religion with about 2.1 billion members worldwide. Its foundation is rooted on the teachings of Jesus Christ who lived 2,000 years ago. Within the Christian faith they are over 250 denominations.

Buddhism is a belief that focuses on personal spiritual development. Buddhism was founded by followers of Siddhartha Gautama in India and is over 2,500 year old. Its belief system is based on the presumption that all life is interconnected and should be respected. People who practice Buddhism do worship a God, but show respect and tolerance for other belief systems. They believe that the path to enlightenment is through the practice of meditation, practising morality and self-denial, and increasing personal knowledge.

Hinduism is also another ancient religion. It is at least 3000 years old. (Colledge, 1999) Hindus believe in a universal God who is called the Brahma (the Creator of all reality); Vishnu or

Krishna is the preserver of all of the creations and Shiva is the destroyer (AllAboutGOD, 2010). Hinduism does not have a founder or identified prophet; the authors of Hinduism's holy books are unnamed. Hindus believe in reincarnation, which includes the cycle of birth, death and rebirth that is governed by Karma. Hinduism has a huge range of popular belief, elaborate ritual and philosophy. Colledge (1999) inform that there are many stages in Hinduism including transition, magic, animal worship, belief in demons, a multitude of Gods of varying degrees of power, mysticism, asceticism, abstract theology, some of which is very profound, plus a variety of esoteric doctrines

Sikhism is a monotheistic religion, established by Hindus in the sixteenth century, and believes in the universal God who is similar to the God worshipped by Christians, Jews and Muslims. Sikhism is the fifth largest world religion, with some 23 million adherents, about four million of whom live in Europe or America. Hinduism and Sikhism have special holy days, dietary rules, and forms of dress. Islam and Judaism also have special holy days, and dietary laws.

3.4 What is Spirituality? How is an understanding of this concept relevant for health care providers?

Spirituality, in a broad sense is a concern with matters of the spirit, and is a wide term with many available readings. It may include belief in supernatural powers, but the emphasis is often on personal experience. For others spirituality leads to the discovery of hope, love, trust compassion and peace in one's life. There are many tools that can be used to discover the true pathway to spirituality. These include connecting with nature, music, art, yoga, meditation, religion, reading inspirational books, relaxation, and attending religious services. Through these activities one can cultivate positive beliefs, improve health and well being, and contemplate life in the hereafter.

Remen (1999) emphasises that spirituality provides the deepest sense of belonging and participation. Thus members of the Pentecostal Christian faith believed that having a personal experience in spirituality can only be attained through the process by which one seeks to be filled by the Holy Ghost. This is done through consistent praying and fasting, resulting in the empowerment of the Holy Ghost. Such experience provides the opportunity to speak in unknown tongues or language, which can be used as vehicle to reveal God's plan for human beings or to forecast a catastrophe that will be imminent. Others who are filled with the Holy Spirit also have the ability to interpret those members who are speaking in tongues. The spirit serves as a protector and guide for the individual towards the pathway of righteousness and holiness.

In many countries, especially in many parts of Africa, individuals, groups or communities believe in spirit possession. In some communities spirits are regarded as evil, good or productive spirits. Belief in spirits and possession is considered to be normal and is accepted by many African communities. The reality of possession by spirits, or for that matter of witchcraft, constitutes an integral part of the total system of religious ideas and assumptions. In Jamaica there is a popular saying that a person who is kind-hearted is considered to be "a good spirited" person, while those who break the law are regarded as "bad spirited" individuals. For a health care setting, spirituality plays a very important part in comforting those who are experiencing illness, bereavement, marriage problems, and melancholy moments in their personal lives.

In terms of mortality, Strawbridge et al (1999) wrote on the basis of observational studies that people who have regular spiritual practices tend to live longer. Patients who are spiritual may utilise their belief in coping with illness, pain and life stresses. Moreover, spiritually connected or comforted individuals or patients tend to have a more positive outlook and quality of life. For example, patients with advanced cancer found comfort from their religious and spiritual beliefs were more satisfied in their lives, were happier.

3.5 How do you work with a Jehovah's Witness patients who refuse a blood transfusion?

Jehovah Witnesses believe that that blood is sacred to God and is beheld in the eyes of God; blood means life and should be seen as holy. Moreover, the faith's members believe that blood should not be eaten or used in any life saving attempt - for example blood transfusion. According to Jehovah's Witness publications, religious and spiritual teaching based on biblical interpretations, in particular the passage: 'You must not eat the blood of any sort of flesh.' (Leviticus 17 v. 14). In addition it is believed that 'Blood was reserved for only one special use, the atonement for sins, which led up to Jesus' shedding of blood (*Awake* 2006 and *The Watch Tower* 1997). Witnesses believe that when a Christian refuses blood he or she is assuring that only the blood of Jesus Christ can cure or safe life. In 2000 the Centre for Studies on New Religion 'CESNUR' reported on the official statement made to the media on matters of Blood Transfusion by Jehovah Witness: 'If one of Jehovah's Witnesses is transfused against his or her will, Jehovah's Witnesses do not believe that this constitutes a sin on the part of the individual'. The Supreme Court of Connecticut upheld the right of a Jehovah's Witness to refuse a blood transfusion.

However, new thinking by Witnesses indicates that blood transfusions have been demoted to "non-disfellowshipping events" meaning that an individual will not be expelled from the religion if they have accepted a blood transfusion. The Human Rights Act of 1998 addressed Freedom of Thought, Conscience and Religion in stating that: *If a court's determination of any question arising under this Act might affect the exercise by a religious organisation (itself or its members collectively) of the right to freedom of thought, conscience and religion, it must have particular regard to the importance of that right.* Based on this principle, the patient has the right to refuse a blood-transfusion. However, Jehovah's Witness parents do not have the right to deny a life-saving blood transfusion for their minor child.

3.6 Rastafarians - if the body is a 'temple', is this the same for their children in hospital?

Rastafarians believe that the body is created by Jah or Jehovah, the Almighty God, and is itself the temple of God. If the body is considered to be the temple, then it is regarded as holy and should not be contaminated by sinful behaviour or by eating certain kind of foods or bi-products of food. The body should not be mentally or physically abused. Unclean consumables are a recipe for contaminating clean bodies. Hence, they refrain from eating meat such as pork, which is considered to be unclean. Some liberal Rastafarians eat chicken, but others refuse to eat products such as eggs, cheese and white flour products. Believers of Rastafarianism follow the religious and spiritual biblical instructions of bible verses in Exodus, Genesis, Proverbs and Leviticus, e.g. "Better is a dinner of herbs where love is." From this standpoint Rastafarians are strict vegetarians, believing (as do many Seventh Day Adventists and Quakers) that God, the Supreme Being dwells within their bodies. This guides Rastafarians to differentiate between good and evil and to nurture their minds towards righteousness – finally achieving the rite of passage to their African homeland, Ethiopia. The body is should be scrupulously cared for, maintained and respected. Acts of homosexuality and sex change are deemed to be sinful, and serve as an agent to contaminate the body or temple created by God. Throughout the Caribbean and in most African countries there is a fearsome persecution of homosexuals and lesbians, whose lifestyles are said to offend scripture (see *Romans I, 8-32*). For African men and women with homosexual and lesbian inclinations, (which ironically, are usually present from childhood in the divinely-created human body), choices are limited and include cultural estrangement, flight as refugees, or suicide (Bagley and Tremblay, 2001).

In the case of children, many Rastafarians sees it as their duty to raise their child in the philosophy of Rastafarianism. Rastafarians should be consulted regarding the nursing and treatment of their children. For example, in the case of blood transfusion some Rastafarians see blood as a source of life, and will not reject a blood transfusion, but will in the first instance need to be assured that the blood is not contaminated with diseased organisms or agents. However, it is important that in nutritional care all foods that are considered to be unclean should not be included in the child's diet.

3.7 How can we approach patients whose religious beliefs require specific medical procedures and care?

In some religions, for example Islam, a female patient may refuse care from a male nurse or doctor. In this case, if a Muslim female patient has gynaecological problems and requests that she be seen by a medical carer of the same gender, efforts should be made to ensure that only a female gynaecologist, obstetrician or nurse specialist should attend this patient. According to an article published the Ethics Department of Catholic Health (2004) on Patient Preferences, the health care institution should support same sex caregivers because they realise a patient's perception of appropriate care. If the request is motivated by modesty or religious tradition (e.g. Islam), or where perception has been demonstrated to improve the quality of care, then accommodating preferences should be considered (Ethics Department of Catholic Health, 2004). In addition, on this question, Shahid Athar, former chair of Medical Ethics of Islamic Medical Association of North America suggested, that if available, same sex health care providers are encouraged but, if not available and in life saving situations, "necessity overrides the prohibition" - a rule of Islamic Shariah law.

Another issue affecting Muslim patients is that of fasting from all solids and liquids during the daylight hours of Ramadan, which may last several weeks in each year. In Northern countries this can mean a fast of up to 15 hours, and this could endanger the health of those with diabetes. There is also some evidence that women's and children's health might be affected by fasting in the early stages of pregnancy. Islam is flexible about this, and those with diabetes, and women who are pregnant are allowed to break their fast on health grounds.

3.8 A female patient from Jamaica, Pakistan or Africa believes her illness to have been caused by a magic spell put on her by a jealous member of the same community. What can we do?

The concept of illness according to Helman (1997) lies in the notion that it can originate from different cultural, physical and psychological aspects of identity, for example the supernatural, natural, social or individual world. The belief system that is presented by the female patient from Pakistan or Africa fits directly into a phenomenon of the supernatural, where the tools of magic, and evil spirits are allegedly used by some malevolent person or force to make a person become ill. Underwood and Underwood (1981) describe spiritual forms of the Islam, which can apparently, cause ill health. Here one needs to examine the difference between cultural belief and values, which contrast sharply with the values of Western medical practice of psychiatry and physical health – the contrast, as Indians term it, between "ayurvedic" and "allopathic" systems of medicine. Gorham (1989) comments that human experience and action reflects five different aspects of identity, for example the mental, physical, social, emotional and spiritual. Although often crucially important, it is sometimes very difficult to recognise.

On the other hand, from the spiritual perspective, a psychiatrist or mental health professional could come to the conclusion that the patient is exhibiting the mode of magical thinking. Thomson and Mathias et al (2000) have argued that it is relatively easy to recognise elements of magical thinking. The thoughts displayed by the patient may appear illogical when they are based on what is alleged to be superstition. The internal, cultural reference points of the patient's identity can, at times of stress, trigger certain behavioural actions, and hence a particular outcome; and in this case the illness of the patient. For the patient, jealousy of a member of the same community can initiate delusional behavioural qualities. In order to address this significant problem, it is important to understand the cultural belief of the individual and to explore various health care strategies that can be used to help the patient overcome their problem.

It seems reasonable that the health practitioner should discuss and develop with the patient, a holistic care model that could offer the nurse an understanding of both mind and body, from a multicultural perspective. To address the issue of supernatural or magical forces, which are believed to cause illness and anxiety, the patient might be referred to a spiritual or cultural healer. For instance, Al-Krenaul and Graham (1999), writing from an Islamic perspective, make reference to Al-Jzari (1987) and Al-Daramdash (1991), who stated that there are several types of healers - an example given is the Koranic healer who has knowledge of the evil spirit's world, and purports to know how evil spirits enter the human body and what might influence them to leave. When it is thought that the patient is occupied by a devil, treatment may consist of beating and starving the patient — either the patient dies (in which case there is no further problem, except when the devil or spirit then occupies another person); or the spirit departs for a more acceptable host. These options obviously present the multicultural health worker with some acute dilemmas, especially when the "infected" person is a child. A milder form of folk treatment is for an Imam to recite passages of the Qur'an into a glass of water, which the patient will then drink, often to good effect. This effect might be real, or it could be down to 'the placebo effect' - but in cross-cultural therapy the patient's belief that the therapy works should be considered as important.

Clients have the right to privacy and confidentiality. Trust and transparency between both psychiatrist and the patient is vital for any care intervention to be successful. Zola (1973) points out that one of the difficulties that doctors experience, in addressing patient problems, arises from the failure to apply treatment with an understanding of popular or folk beliefs. Thus, addressing the hypothetical case of the Pakistani or African female patient should be done from a holistic perspective, considering where the cultural beliefs and values might play important role in planning and providing the right care model. A cross-cultural care model in this case might be ideal for the patient.

3.9 Why do some people in the African Caribbean culture put a gold pin in the feet of their dead partner?

This practice is based on the cultural notion that a deceased soul or spirit wanders the earth for forty days and forty nights, and during that time the spirit has a tendency to visit the residential homes where they once lived. In addition, it is believed that during the visit they exhibit sexual behaviour, and may approach their spouse. The insertion of an object in the feet of the deceased prevents the deceased spirit from walking because of the pain they would experience. The control and management of the deceased spirit is vital for the mental health of relatives, and also prevents the telling of negative stories about the deceased in the community. Vassel (2006) observed that the belief that newly deceased spirits are confused and weak, as they have not yet found their spiritual place of rest. They are the favourites of spirits who wish to use them to be used for obeah, witchcraft or black magical purposes. They can be summoned from the burial ground by obeah man used to carry out task of the obeah person. All of these beliefs and rituals clash with Christian beliefs and rituals. However, a small number of people in the African-Caribbean population may hold dual beliefs in both Animism and Christianity.

Miller (2002) explained that 'Obeah' or 'Guzu' is the belief that there are paranormal forces that can be used for good or evil, for health or sickness. Obeah workers (witchcraft) are believed to have the skills to create conditions, through which one's desires (and fears and nightmares) can be fulfilled.

For instance, they can cause illness, death, separation, divorce, love and prosperity. According to Miller, any illness or sickness that cannot be explained by medical intervention in the community might be considered to be a result of obeah or witchcraft. If the person's illness is believed to be induced by obeah, the victim is generally taken to a "balm yard" or mission, which is the holy ground of the Pocomania religion, to undergo a ritual. This could involve exorcism or the using of herbs and special oils for healing the patient. However, notions of witchcraft and of Pocomania are likely to be rare in the African Caribbean community in Britain, although there is no academic study of this.

Similarly, African religious rituals of using children's body parts for healing are notably absent in Britain, apart from the case of the murdered child called 'Adam', whose mutilated body was found floating in the river Thames – the true identity of this dismembered child was never discovered. Forensic analysis showed that Adam, aged about 10 years, had been killed through the forced ingestion of a paste of the calabar bean, laced with gold, causing paralysis, which enabled the witchcraft practitioners to remove organs while Adam was still conscious, alive and experiencing 'extreme pain' – an important part of the ritual (Owen, 2009). The gold was probably a propitiation of the boy's spirit. Forensic analysis showed that Adam had been born and lived in Benin City, Nigeria and had recently been brought to Britain. Owen estimated that each year hundreds of children in Africa are ritually killed for purposes of healing adults and warding off evil spirits, but Adam is the only known case in Europe.

Clearly, this is a form of "spiritual healing" which we would not advocate.

SECTION 4: DIABETIS, SEXUAL HEALTH, MENTAL HEALTH

4.1 How can we advise people about their Type 2 diabetes if we don't know their cultural habits?

The nurse practitioners or health care professionals, who are caring for people with diabetes, should have basic cultural information about the clients for whom they are providing a service. Being aware of the patient's cultural background, may provide the platform for effective communication between the patient and the care staff. Papadopoulos and Lees (2004) write that humans are all cultural beings – this is reflected in their shared beliefs, values, norms, communication, and language. Culture is handed down from generation to generation and during this transmission process, people change as individuals meet and exchange information within the cultural melting pot. This information exchange has the ability to impact on a person's way of life, attitudes and behavioural practices in the environment and community in which they reside.

Triandis (1977) suggests that culture can be seen from an objective point of view, and this can be tangible: for example the food people eat. Helman (1997) observes that the meals people eat, can be used to symbolise social as well as cultural status. This can determine the type and quality of food of the individual, in order to identify them with a class hierarchy, or type of religion. Since culture is about knowledge, habits, skills, and attitudes (that have been passed down by example), and the processes of socialisation (for example in family or group); in holistic terms culture represents the identity of the group that is accepted implicitly or explicitly, and to a greater or lesser degree by it members. Individuals, who act out these cultural indicators, may do so unconsciously because it represents a learned behaviour. This has important implications for the health carer's understanding, to be aware of the cultural eating habit of their clients, in order to advise them on the importance of management of their diabetes. According to Papadopoulos and Lees (2004) and Campinha-Bacote (1998), cultural awareness, sensitivity, competence, skills and knowledge encounters are key components of cultural competence, which enable health practitioners to address issues surrounding the cultural habits of patients and clients. But the health practitioner should also be aware that not all members of an ethnic group adhere to the same set of cultural standards (e.g. in groups with cultural origins in India and Pakistan, those who are Christians, Moslems and Hindus may have fundamentally different sets of values). Younger generations may have largely adopted the cultural values of their indigenous peers – especially true of the growing number of young people who marry across ethnic or "racial" boundaries.

In the United Kingdom it is recorded that ethnic minority groups, such as African Caribbean and

Asians are the groups with the highest percentage of diabetic disease (especially Type 2 Diabetes), when compared with the indigenous population. The Kings College London (2006) report on Diabetes Mellitus, suggests that 'about three in every 100 people in the UK are believed to have diabetes and more than over three-quarters of these will have Type 2 diabetes.'

Doll et al (2004) and Bahr (2001) have suggested that life-styles can cause illnesses such as Type 2 Diabetes. It follows that health carers need to comprehend various cultural forces, which have an impact on the life styles of individuals, and how these contribute to the development of diabetes in certain groups. Additional factors such as poverty, low wages, unemployment, health care access, educational inequalities, racial discrimination, poor diet and exercise, stress, poor communication skills, mental health problems, poor knowledge of how diabetes is caused, religion, and spirituality, amongst other factors - all play a significant role in the development of Type 2 diabetes. All of these factors may contribute to the way of life of the individual and the outcome of diabetes. Patient education about diabetes and strategies to deal with poverty and malnutrition are tools to be used to increase diabetes awareness amongst clients.

4.2 What can we do to modify or accommodate the eating and cooking habits of ethnic minorities, especially African Caribbean/Asian populations, since they are the groups with highest incidence of Diabetes Type 2 in the United Kingdom?

The challenge of changing ethnic minority cooking or eating habits is a consistently difficult task for health professionals. Food beliefs and practices of various groups are a result of historical, cultural, social, religious or spiritual factors. Afro-Caribbean sometimes see their food as cultural food, which identifies them with their ancestors' nutrition and eating habits. From their perspective, food can also be classified as strong or weak, and this can determine whether a person becomes physically and mentally strong, in order to deal with the hardships of life; or the individual can become weak without the ability to ward off diseases, and remain free from illnesses.

Many of the older generation of Afro-Caribbean believe that yam, cocoa, dasheen, sweet potato, cassava, breadfruit baddoe, banana and flour dumplings are *strong* foods; responsible for providing the body with energy and increasing body size. These foods (rich in carbohydrates) are classified as energy giving foods, which are responsible for maintaining and building the body's strength and appearance. Vegetables such as cabbage and lettuce are identified as weak foods, because after eating them the individual becomes hungry quite quickly. In addition, some

Afro-Caribbean's eat certain types of food based on their religious belief. For example, those who identify with Seventh day Adventism will abstain from food that the bible identifies as unclean, so they will abstain from pork and pork products as well as shell fish, but will eat milk, cheese and milk foods. Many Adventists, seeking to "preserve the body as a holy temple", are vegetarians. Adventists will not consume alcohol or drinks containing caffeine.

From an Asian perspective religion and also geographical region influences the kinds of food eaten. Sheikh and Thomas (1994) for example, explained that Punjabis and Mirpuris from North West India and Pakistan, base their diet mainly on wheat products but also consume ghee, which is calcified butter, to prepare vegetables. On the other hand, Asians who identify themselves as Gujaratis mainly eat wheat, chapattis, millet and vegetables – most people from Gujarat are vegetarian. Bengali groups consume likes to mainly rice and fish.

Religion plays a direct role in the eating habit of Muslims, Hindus, Sikhs and others. For instance a Muslim will follow the dietary rules which are also followed by most Jews, regarding abstinence from pork, and eating only meat killed in a ritual manner "free from blood" (as required by Leviticus - kosher and halal meat products are very similar, and derive from the same biblical passages, since both Judaism and Islam are "religions of the book" i.e. the Old Testament). Hindus will abstain from beef and many Indian vegetarians will not even eat eggs.

African Caribbean and Asians often like to prepare their food with a spicy taste or flavour; this includes seasoning salt, peppers, herbs and spices. Food will be freshly cooked and eaten throughout the day. Also, it is expected that during visitation by families and friends, giving meals is an important part of entertaining. During the holy month of Ramadan, Muslims will fast from food and water during daylight hours, breaking their fast at night time by eating dates, followed by substantial cooked meals at night and in the early morning.

All religious and cultural groups need to develop sets of dietary guidelines, which are both compatible with custom and with religious prescription, but also give excellent nutrition in a way which does not cause obesity or high blood sugar levels. It is very important that cultural food beliefs are not neglected in the education of patients, while emphasis is placed on the need to moderately consume a variety of foods, which will prevent individuals developing diabetes. One of the tools that could be used, to change or improve the cooking and health belief practices of ethnic minority groups, is a programme centred on health nutrition and literacy. This should be designed, in collaboration and partnership with community ethnic groups, and presented in local dialects and languages, using visual role plays to educate people in local community centres.

4.3 Why are some ethnic minority patients reluctant about taking insulin by self-injection and prefer a nurse to administer the injection?

Davis and Renda (2006) point out that for patients with Type 2 diabetes, insulin injections are often linked with several negative associations. These may include feeling a sense of loss of control or management over one's life, a reduction in the quality of life, failure to control diabetes, side effects such as weight gain and hypoglycaemia, and daily, possibly painful, injections. They suggest that it is not surprising that many patients with Type 2 diabetes are reluctant to start insulin therapy. Based on this interpretation, there are many reasons why some African Caribbean (among others) are reluctant to self-medicate by injection, and would prefer another person to do this. This could involve issues of identity, self confidence, mental health, anxiety, fear in making mistakes, horror of self-inflicted pain, damage to skin or body and fear of needles. In addition, lack of knowledge on how to self-medicate correctly, concerns about developing abscesses, upholding the belief that oral forms of medication are more effective - all of these factors can lead to the patient to feeling embarrassed or hopeless, and hence reliant on the nurse.

Cox and Stone (2006) expressed the idea that: 'Difficulties with self-injection, including inability to self-inject, are common for individuals taking home-administered injectable medications'. In addition, Polonosky and Jackson (2004) observed that 'Patients do not feel they can manage the demands of insulin therapy, and also insulin is associated with a perceived loss of control over one's life'. This is certainly true, in the author's experience, of some Afro-Caribbean patients who become reluctant to self-medicate by injection, because of self-blame or feeling guilty because of the illness or disease. Moreover, some Afro Caribbeans believe that the body could heal itself of disease (given an adequate diet) and hence, see another reason for not taking prescribed medication. Furthermore, from a religious belief point of view, an Afro Caribbean patient may believe in a miracle, willed by the creator who will heal the body of a chosen few, from diseases.

On the other hand, the patient may be able to tolerate the procedure carried out by a professional, because of trust and confidence and hence their dependency on the nurse. It is believed that nurses are trained to administer injections and errors or mistakes are minimal. To deal with the problem of the reluctant sufferer of diabetes, it is vital that individuals are educated about the risk of non-compliance. They should be advised about the health and related problems that may be experienced, if medication (including insulin injections) and good diet are avoided. Complications which have a high frequency in diabetes Type 2 sufferers include cardiovascular disease, kidney damage (leading to renal failure), limb amputation, blindness, numbness (leading to insensitivity and to pain), pressure in the feet, development of heart and stroke disease and other complications - not infrequent complications of inadequately treated diabetes. Effort should be made to encourage motivation by directing clients to local diabetic groups or clubs. Addressing the issues of pain, fear, stress, anxiety or psychological problems of patients, who have a phobia of needles, should be done in consultation with a psychotherapist. On the theme of religious belief, the patient should be encouraged to see their local pastors or spiritual leaders for advice.

4.4 What are some of the emotional and behavioural consequences we would expect from a person when they are first told that   they have a serious health problem, for example diabetes?

The reactions of an individual, who has recently discovered they have a serious health problem, may be expressed within a physical, cultural, social, emotional, spiritual or religious domain. Helman (1997) suggests that stress can arise even from usually positive experiences such as promotion, engagement, marriage, the birth of a child or winning a lottery, all of which involve a change of life style. We are reminded by Helman that individual behaviour varies in coping with life change situations. From a religious perspective the individual may change his way of life and focus, in order to practice personal rituals appropriately, as well as the need to prepare oneself to meet God in case of a terminal disease; or hoping for spiritual assurance that the disease they experience can be removed through divine healing. Such spiritual aspirations are expressed by using prayers, fasting and telling people about the good role that God plays in their lives. For believers in God, preparation of their spiritual soul is of the uttermost importance as this is a necessary (but not sufficient) precursor of entry into heaven or into a higher realm of rebirth. Some individuals will display particular emotional behavioural qualities. Teijlingen (2003) defines emotion "… as subjective feelings or states experienced by individuals, but not observable by others, although associated physical manifestation may give away the emotion to an observer." Such emotional manifestation may be observed in the denial of the reality of a disease. The Community Alcohol Information Program (CAIP, 1997) explains that:

> *Denial is the psychological process by which human beings protect themselves from things which threaten them, by blocking knowledge of those things from their awareness. It is a defence, which distorts reality; it keeps us from feeling the pain and uncomfortable truth about things we do not want to face. If we cannot feel or see the consequences of our actions, then everything is fine and we can continue to live without making any changes. (CAIP 1997)*

In this case the individual refuses to accept that the validity of a test that verifies the development of the disease. The patient may refuse to accept the results given by the health professional. The individual may say that they feel fine and healthy, and state that nothing is wrong with them. On the other hand, some clients will be engaging in the process of intellectualisation by being involved in extensive research (e.g. on the web), to find out the reasons for the development of the disease and how they can go about curing it themselves, with diet and folk remedies. In traditional Caribbean culture they might visit the 'Balm Yard', in a local setting where they would contact local traditional healers to participate in healing and purification ceremonies. This will consist of fusion of medicinal bush or herb products used to prepare a bath for the individual. Balm yards are popular places in the island of Jamaica, although there number is unknown in Britain. Some patients will not follow orthodox medical instructions for taking medication for their problems, believing that they might cause weight gain, interfere with sexual performance, or make their illness worst. Given the listed side effects of many prescribed medications, this may not be an entirely irrational belief! Others will refuse to follow nutritional advice for their diabetic condition, fearing that they will not be able to eat cultural food in their family setting, with the fear being isolated by community members during festivities.

4.5 How can we care for an Asian vegetarian with diabetes, who has communication problems, particularly with regard to explaining appropriate diet and insulin treatment?

The term 'Asian' includes several sub groups of people that could include Muslims, Sikhs, Indian and Nepali Hindus, East African Gujarati Hindus, Pakistani and Bangladeshi Muslims and others. Each group has different religions (or variations of the same religion), including Buddhists, Muslims, Hindus and other groups, all with varying spirituality, beliefs and practices. The Asian, who is vegetarian and whose first language is not English, may need a health care interpreter to convey health information. This can be quite difficult as the person's religious and spiritual practices may have a profound importance for health practices and diet. It is very important to note how religious practices can significantly influence what a person eats, or the expected time or period in which they are required to take their insulin medication. Nutrition and diet should be planned with relatives. If the patient feels that he/she is not able to participate in what is prepared in the home, this can create psychological problems for the patient, as from a cultural view point it is expected that everyone should dine together. In some family gatherings and from a cultural stand point this can lead to isolation of the patient.

On the other hand using interpreters can be problematic, as some patients may be reluctant in giving intimate details to a non-medical person. It is important that the patient is told to provide someone who they can trust to receive the information on their behalf, which would then be translated in the language of their choice. Diets for Sikhs, Muslims, Buddhists, Christians and Hindus vary, so a good understanding is essential to ensure that planned diet care is adhered to in order to keep the disease in control. A large hospital will employ a consultant dietician, and he or she may be consulted about individual cases. If the patient is illiterate, then it is vital that the patient's relative or friend (with the patient's permission) is included as part of the briefing team. It is also important for the nurse to be able to communicate with the patient from a trans-cultural perspective. Learning key words used in the patient's first language will ease the difficulty of communicating, but it is always best to use a translator.

Using insulin made from animals, such as pigs, will not be acceptable for many groups and a suitable alternative should be used. For a vegetarian (or a Hindu), using insulin derived from bovine or other animal sources should be avoided. Drugs which will stimulate the pancreas to produce appropriate amounts of insulin, as well as careful dieting and weight control should be tried, if the patient's cultural background means that injected insulin offends religious prescriptions. There are now biochemical breakthroughs, which mean that insulin for injection can be synthetically produced, using plants rather than animals.

Ultimately however, the patient and their relatives may be faced with the alternatives: using insulin to avoid disability and death *versus* offending traditional cultural and religious values. Information about diabetes should be provided in the patient language for example in Urdu, Punjabi, Gujarati, Bengali, Arabic, Cantonese and other languages. Patients, who cannot understand verbal or written English, are almost always elderly people who immigrated to Britain later in life – for example, elderly Cantonese from Hong Kong.

4.6 How can we get the message across that wearing a condom during sexual activity is important in reducing Sexual Transmitted Infections (STIs) in Afro-Caribbean Communities?

This question is not only pertinent to Afro-Caribbean communities but also to a diverse community that includes many different ethnic groups. It important that sexual health experts comprehend various behavioural habits of individual group, which may reflect the cultural beliefs and practices that are shared between individuals within the community and across a variety of mixed community groups or setting. Transforming sexual behaviour requires resources and commitment. The writer understands that many Afro-Caribbean, who choose not to wear a condom during sexual intercourse, base this behaviour on the view that this reduces sensitivity and sexual pleasure.

Others base their decision not to wear a condom

on religious and spiritual groundings - that the spermatozoa is a gift from God and any act to destroy the semen results in committing a spiritual crime. The punishment allocated to this is spiritual death. It is also the comprehension of the author that some females share the same belief – that any form of female contraception reduces the pleasure of sex, and their emotional communication with their partners. In addition, some individuals feel that the spermatocide, which is found within some condoms, has the ability to cause loss of sensation of the glan-penis, or indeed might cause cancer of the penis or cervix. (Ironically, unprotected sex can cause cancer of the cervix, passed in the form of viruses from man to woman).

In sexual health education, effective communication is a vital tool in getting the message across to promote the philosophy of safe sex in diverse communities. There are many challenges in promoting sexual health education - for example tackling personal belief systems and peer pressure, manhood issues, myths about sexual abilities and dealing with curiosity, ignorance and experimentation. Ultimately, there is much to be gained in teaching and following the precepts of traditional religion, which are affirmed (formally at least) by the large majority of Afro-Caribbean: completed sex before and outside of marriage constitutes fornication and adultery. Moral rules and the welfare of others must take precedence over the selfish pursuit of personal sexual pleasure.

An effective strategy that needs to be implemented is one that seeks to encourage sexual health education in the community, schools, religious and spiritual institutions, through the process of collaboration and partnership of health agencies, as well as community and religious organisations. Morrissey (1998) argues that 'Society is preoccupied by sexuality, taking it very seriously, but rarely attempting to consider it rationally.' He says that sexuality – prowess and pleasure - has become the medium through which many people define their personalities, establish their personalities, establish identities and become conscious of themselves.

Reflecting from an Afro-Caribbean perspective: some believe that to be a man and macho means that one should be sexually active, taking risks and enjoying sexual encounters. Some even view the manufacturing of condoms, by business organisations as a financial strategy, to exploit the poor through making profits and a conspiracy to reduce the birth rate of global black population. On the other hand sexual health educators, such as Pratt (2003) see promoting the concept on positive sexuality - for example, as having sexual information and developing knowledge in relation to sexual and reproductive phenomena - is associated with healthier sexuality and higher self esteem, respect for self and others, non- exploitive sexual satisfaction, and the capacity to enjoy and control sexual and reproductive behaviour in accordance with social and personal ethics. Awareness of sexually transmitted infections should be at forefront of any sexual health campaign.

The effects of being infected with HIV/AIDS,

gonorrhoea, syphilis, herpes or Chlamydia results in altered body image, urethral and vaginal discharge or genital ulceration, and should be discussed with vigour and dedication. Laverack (2004) sees the benefits of community development, a concept that is based on educating the individual within groups, within the broader community. However, he warns that the westernised community philosophy is often expressed in individualistic terms. Within a diverse society, each community groups have the right to community integrity, with their own system of behaviours, in contrast with those who originated from the East, Africa and from other countries, which have a different interpretation of what community empowerment contains.

Erzinger (1994) confirms this in his argument, that community empowerment is often more concerned with the family or extended kin system. It is important to work through effective community actions in setting priorities, making decisions, planning strategies, and implementing them to achieve better health (WHO 1986). Thus the precedence is to focus on engaging group commitment, community interactions, partnership and collaboration with community and kinship groups, giving them "ownership" of sexual health strategies.

4.7 A patient suffering from mental health problems said that every time he looks at the nurse, he sees horns coming out of the nurse's head. How might one deal with a patient's delusional beliefs?

It is likely that the patient is experiencing visual hallucinations, which can reflect a variety of causes ranging from drug and alcohol intoxication, states of fever, epileptic 'aura' (particularly associated with temporal lobe epilepsy) through to a full psychotic state, which could be temporary, or part of a longer-term mental health problem. Hallucinations are defined by Varcarolis (2006) as sensory perceptions for which there is no apparent external stimulus; and the most common types of hallucination are auditory (hearing sounds), visual (seeing persons or things) olfactory (smelling odours), gustatory (experiencing taste), and tactile (feeling bodily sensation). Lyttle (1986) also suggests that the hallucinating person is one who is experiencing false perceptions occurring in the absence of an eternal stimulus. This pseudo perception of sight may manifest itself in many ways - for example, the individual may see people as giants, they also may visualise various shapes, and objects, animals or flashes of light. In other cases, according to a person suffering from hallucinations, they may see an individual as Lilliputian, which is a reduction in size of the person.

Observers have noticed that Lilliputian

hallucinations are sometimes reported by people who are ill with cholera, malaria, typhoid or scarlet fever. If the patient is also suffering from mental health problems, it is not unusual for them to experience visual hallucinations Varcarolis (2006) - particularly if a person's central nervous system may have undergone physical or neurological damage because of febrile illness, an injury involving CNS trauma or following a head injury acquired in various ways. The health care worker should not assume that the hallucinating person is 'mad', or suffering a major psychosis. This could be the case, but proper referral and assessment is crucial.

A nurse experiencing a communication from a patient, about a delusion or hallucination that perhaps implies paranoia can themselves experience anxiety, stress, fear and de-motivation. It is vital that the nurse remains positive in his or her role as professional, which is to provide the best care for the patient in the clinical setting. To feel insecure in dealing with the problem may result in the nurse adopting defensive behaviours, such as withdrawal and avoidance, manifested as low self confidence and hopelessness in their duties. The best way of addressing this problem is to report these concerns to managers, seeking a mentor who will offer guidance and to seek (or provide) further professional education. The nurse can improve his or her knowledge and skill by seeking knowledge updates, attending courses, seminars and workshops on the topic. The professional carer or nurse should be aware that the hallucinations are real to the person who is experiencing them and, when approaching the patient should do so in manner which is nonthreatening and non-judgemental (Moller and Murphy 2002). Remember, when a patient is experiencing hallucinations, these are likely to be associated with fear and anxiety.

It is recommended by Varcarolis (2006) that the nurse should call the person by name, speaking simply and non-judgementally. The nurse could offer reassuring messages to the patient. For example, Dr. Ari Querido, a Dutch social psychiatrist, uses the "crossed wires" reassurance model, telling the patient that the brain, a very complex organ, has numerous electrical pathways, and a simple malfunction can result in false messages, hearing voices, seeing things which others cannot, etc. (Pilgrim and Rogers, 2002). This, within the context of a cognitive restructuring programme, can help the patient to "rise above" the phenomenon of false perceptions.

However, dealing with this illness is challenging as it can be one of the markers for dementia, as in for example, Alzheimer's disease. The nurse should ensure that the patient is seen by a psychiatrist, neurologist or geriatrician, who will be able to prescribe appropriate medication or refer the patient to a psychotherapist, who can teach the patient coping skills, probably within the framework of cognitive restructuring, with appropriate medication.

4.8 Can we explain the difference between psychological, spiritual, social and cultural pain from a mental health perspective?

Generally, Perry and Potter (2004) states that 'pain' is a complex phenomenon that is much more than a single sensation caused by a specific stimulus. The stimulus for pain can be physical and/or mental in nature. Pain is subjective and can be highly individualised.

Psychological pain can be classed as pain due to psychological stress, or outcomes of traumatic experiences that alters the behavioural qualities of the individual, for example in the family, social or interpersonal settings. For example, constant headache can cause tension, inability to concentrate, sweating, tight breathing or trembling and can have a significant effect on the self-confidence and long-term mental health of the individual. Indeed, many neuroses manifest themselves in a physical manner, so that cause and effect may be difficult to untangle. The person experiencing chronic (but often mild negative symptoms) may present themselves as tearful, fearful, anxious and socially isolated. WiseGeek (2010) concludes that 'psychological pain' is a form of mental suffering.

In the case of spiritual pain, if a person believes that they have lost connection with God or the Creator, they may express feelings of fearfulness, condemnation of self, anger, restlessness or depression. These factors can be noted as emotional expression which may lead to a change in ritual behaviours, such as continuous fasting and prayer. Other actions may result in isolation from spiritual and religious groups and entry into a spiritual void, in which God's very existence is denied by the chronically ill person.

Some groups believe that God is the creator and this eternal and supernatural force creates all life forms. God's role, in this case, is to show human beings spiritual pathways for proper conduct in relation to self and others. But a chronically suffering (and depressed) individual may express the view that God has deserted them – when more properly we might say that they have deserted God. God will not protect us from illness or accident, but does give human beings the ability to avoid risk, to learn to care for others medically and socially, and to co-operate with health systems in optimising treatment. Prayer to God may tell us how to bear illness, how to avoid illness (e.g. by avoiding alcohol, drugs and tobacco, and risky sexual behaviours). An individual, expressing the idea that God has deserted them, because of the belief that God has failed to protect them from sickness or has failed to cure their illness, is following a false and ultimately selfish, spiritual pathway.

Social pain can be experienced by individuals who have been excluded from society - for example, because of the stigma and discrimination when others know that a person has been diagnosed with a psychiatric illness, Bagley and King (2005). This may result in a person becoming reclusive and not able to participate in community activities.

This in turn can result in hardship and economic problems. A psychiatric diagnosis may lead to a person not being selected as a marital partner in an 'arranged marriage' system. These individuals may actually be disowned by their extended family. The need to be belong to identifiable groups give a sense of security, long term family commitment, communication and when this is lost, the individual may express feelings of hopelessness, frustration and loss of identity.

In understanding 'cultural pain', including forced isolation from one's reference group, one must examine the role of culture in groups. According to Helman (1997), 'culture' consists of knowledge, beliefs, art and music unique to the cultural group, particular types of morality, canon (religious) law, customs and folkways. In addition, Keesing (1981) suggested that a unique culture consists of shared idea, a system of concepts and rules and meanings that underlie social actions, which are expressed in the way that human beings live. Hence individuals who are Sikhs, Muslims, Jews, Hindus, and Christians within Asian, African and Afro-Caribbean groups or sub groups, may have unique sets of cultural values and rituals, habits, types of knowledge, skills and attitudes that characterise the uniqueness of the group.

Immigrants who move to another country may not be able to practise fully the lifestyles that give them their unique identity. Integrating into a society means that one often has to compromise certain behaviours and emotional expressions. When this 'cultural retreat' or 'cultural alienation' becomes a burden for an individual, (perhaps allied with discrimination in the occupational sphere as well) then the concern or pressures experienced can result in cultural pain. In this case, the individual may become depressed or seek out communities that share his or her cultural practices for examples, dress, religion, diet, gender relationships and so on. Thus in the second generation, there may be a retreat into more conservative forms of traditional culture. In the third generation, however, pressures from the educational system, especially from the general peer culture, may cause retreat into culturally alienated lifestyles, which might involve drug use and minor forms of rebellion, including petty crime (Bagley and Al-Refai, 2008).

4.9   Is there a link between mental health and   spiritual issues?

There are many interpretations offered by health psychologists and psychiatrists in this regard. People in the profession tend to agree that mental health is a positive state of mind, and one in which the individual should display responsibility, being self aware, self directive and interacting with others in a worry free manner, which reduces internal and interpersonal tensions. Good mental health (to which spiritual awareness and support can make a large contribution), can be interpreted as the ability to enjoy productive activities, enjoying the interpersonal relationships which are engendered through interactions in church, mosque, temple of synagogue. Also spiritual self-awareness has the ability to encourage individuals to engage in rational thinking, good communication skills, emotional growth, resilience and higher self esteem.

The concept of the spiritual often involves the belief that there is a supernatural force or higher power who governs, in compassion and mercy, all creatures of the earth both great and small. God is believed to be a spirit and hence communication with God or Jehovah is done through prayer. The notion of spirituality is based on the individual's belief system that gives a purpose to life, and a purpose in meeting life's challenges. In the relationship with God it would be vain, and indeed blasphemous, to seek a personal miracle which would cure one's illness. Rather if God calls you to Him, as a spiritual person you must lovingly accept God's will. Each of us has a soul, which in the religious belief system survives death to continue its journey through birth and rebirth, until ultimately the soul is united with God. According to many belief systems, God "puts us to the test" and it is our duty, our privilege, to suffer gladly the trials we are faced with. The cheerful manner in which we both accept and challenge a current illness, co-operating fully with the medical staff who try to cure us, will ultimate count as a blessing.

The individual who is experiencing mental health problems may believe that praying to God will make them well again. But becoming well involves a state of spiritual peace that is driven by the divine spark within us, through our own will, and not through some arbitrary intervention by the divine power. Also in other circumstances, individuals who are experiencing isolation, hopelessness, insecurity, loss of self esteem and confidence may reach out (or be enabled to do so by others) to God with the desire for spiritual peace.

Some African Caribbean patients abstain from food and ask forgiveness through prayer. This is thought to purify the soul, which may bring them, closer to life in God's heavenly kingdom. It is vital that the health practitioner understands the importance of religion and spirituality in the life of the patient who is experiencing mental health problems. The recognition of spiritual (as opposed to physical) healing must be understood by the nurse as part of the cultural recognition, and the development of the psychological and emotional well being of the patient. Thus it is important for the nurse to be aware of the spiritual and religious background of the patient. The health worker must of course respect the patient's particular belief system, including those who are agnostics or atheists. Religious ministers who visit the hospital - the Imam, Priest, Minister, Rabbi or Hindu Pundit - should be consulted. We must accept that individuals will use these spiritual advisors and intermediaries in time of depression, anger, sadness, fear and guilt, often reaching out to supernatural forces or to their image or understanding of God: the deity will soothe the spirit, though this deity will not intervene in the body's organic decay or sickness. But the soul does not depend for its existence on the body's biology.

The health care worker must strive to "cure sometimes" but "comfort always" (Cayley, 1992). Cayley (following Ivan Illich, 1975) gives three principles for the health care worker: seek to understand the patient's agenda; stand in their shoes; and strive for an "I-thou" relationship

(Buber, 1970). This involves "loving your patient as yourself". Remember, it is a spiritual privilege to be able to offer health care to fellow human beings – it is part of *your* journey towards salvation: do it well, with understanding, tolerance, dedication and with love.

Bibliography

Akbar, N (1996) *Breaking the Chains of Psychological Slavery*. Florida: Mind Production Associates

Al-Daramdash, H. (1991) *The Koran as a Treatment Tool for People who are attacked by Satan*. Cairo: Daar Wali-Al-Islamih (In Arabic)

Al-Jzari, A. (1987) *Methods of Prevention of Jinn and Satan*, Cairo: Islamic University Press (In Arabic)

Al-Krenaul, A. and Graham, J.R. (1999) Social work and Quranic mental health healers. *International Social Work*, New York: Sage Publishers.

Al-Refai, N. And Bagley, C. (2008) *Citizenship Education: The British Muslim Perspective*. Rotterdam: Sense Educational Books.

AllAboutGOD (2010) All about Religion, http://www.allaboutreligion.org/common/aboutus.htm

Ansley, F. L. (1997) White supremacy (and what we should do about it) In: R. Delgado & J. Stefancic (Eds) *Critical White Studies: Looking Behind the Mirror.* Philadelphia: Temple University Press.

Bagley, C. (1973) *The Dutch Plural Society: A Comparative Study in Race Relations.* London: Oxford University Press.

Bagley, C. and Al-Refai, N. (2008) Mental health problems of South Asian populations in Britain. In N. Al-Refai and Bagley, C. *Citizenship Education*. Rotterdam: Sense Publishers.

Bagley, C. And King, M. (2005) Exploration of three stigma scales in 83 users of mental health services: implications for campaigns to reduce stigma. *Journal of Mental Health*, 14, 343-256.

Bagley, C. and Mallick, K. (1998) Field dependence, cultural context and academic achievement. *British Journal of Educational Psychology*, 68, 581-587.

Bagley, C. And Tremblay, P. (2001) Elevated rates of suicidal behaviour in gay, lesbian and bisexual youth. *Crisis: Journal of Crisis Intervention and Suicide Studies*, 21, 111-118.

Bagley, C., Van Huizen, A. & Young, L. (1997) Multi-ethnic marriage and interculturalism in Britain and The Netherlands, In D. Woodrow et al. (Eds.) *Intercultural Education: Theories, Policies and Practice*. Aldershot: Ashgate.

Bagley, C. And Verma, G. (1979) *Racial Prejudice, the Individual and Society*. Aldershot: Ashgate.

Bagley, C., Verma, G., Mallick, K. & Young, L. (1979) *Personality, Self-Esteem and Prejudice*. Aldershot: Ashgate.

Bagley, C. and Young, L. (1988) Evaluation of color and ethnicity in young children in Jamaica, Ghana, England and Canada, *International Journal of Intercultural Relations*, 12, 45-60.

Bahr R .(2001) Sports Medicine. *British Medical Journal*, 323, 328-331.

Banton, M. (1987) *Racial Theories*. Cambridge: Cambridge University Press.

Barratt, N. (2009) *WDYTA? Series Three: Celebrity Gallery – Colin Jackson.* www.bbc.co.uk/familyhistory/

Billington, R., Hockey, J. Strawbridge, S. (1998) Exploring Self and Society, Basingstoke Palgrave Macmillan.

Blaut, J.(1992) 'The Theory of Cultural Racism', *Antipode: A Radical Journal of Geography*, Volume 23, p 289-299.

Bradley, M. (1991) *The Iceman Inheritance,*

Prehistoric Sources of Western Man: Racism, Sexism and Aggression. New York: Kayode Publications.

Bonnett, A. (1997) Constructions of whiteness in European and American anti-racism. In P. Werbner & T. Modood (Eds) *Debating Cultural Hybridity: Multi-Cultural Identities and the Politics of Anti-Racism*. London: Zed Books.

Buber, M. (1947/2002) *Between Man and Man*. London: Routledge.

Burgess, S. (2010) *Teacher Bias Against African Caribbean Pupils? Evidence from Exam Moderation*. Bristol: Centre for Market and Public Organisation, University of Bristol.

Burrell, B. (1996) Nine night: death and dying in Jamaica - death rituals in Jamaica, www.findarticles.com/p/articles/

CAIP (1997) The *Community Information Program*. http://www.nh-dwi.com/directns.htm

Campinha-Bacote, J. (1999) *The Process of Cultural Competence in the Delivery Health care Services: A culturally competent Model of Care*. 3rdedition, Cincinnati, OH: Transcultural C.A.R.E. Associates.

Campinha-Bacote, J. (1999) A model and Instrument for addressing cultural competence in health care. *Journal of Nursing Education*, 38 (5) 203-207.

Carew J (1988) *Columbus and the Origins of Racism*. Nottingham, Institute of Race Relations.

Cavalli-Sforza, L. L. (2000) *Genes, Peoples and Languages*. London: Allen Lane, The Penguin Press.

Cayley, D. (1992) *Ivan Illich*. Concord, ONT: Anansi Press.

Cesnur (2000) *Jehovah's Witnesses: Official*

Statement to the Media on Blood Transfusions, http://www.cesnur.org

Christian, M. (2002) *Black Identity in the 20th Century, Expression of the US and UK African Diaspora*. London: Hansib Publications.

Coard, B. (1971) *How the West Indian child is made educationally subnormal in the British school system*. London, New Beacon Books.

Coker N (2001) *Racism in Medicine: Agenda for Change*. London: Kings Fund Publishers.

Colledge, R. (1999) Mastering World Religions, Macmillan Masrer Series, London, Macmillan Press Ltd

Cox, D and Stone J. (2006) Managing self-injection difficulties in patients with relapsing-remitting multiple sclerosis. *Journal of Neuroscience Nursing*, 38, 167-171.

Craig, G. (2009). *Institutional Racism is Still Alive and Thriving in Britain*. Hull: Centre for Social Justice and Inclusion, University of Hull.

Davis, S. and Renda, S. (2006) Psychological insulin resistance: overcoming barriers to insulin therapy. *Diabetes Education*, Suppl. 4, 146S-152S.

Diane L. Adams (Ed.). (1995) *Health Issues for Women of Colour: A Cultural Diversity Perspective*. London: Sage Publications.

Darwin, C. (1859) On the Origin of Species, Penguin, Harmondsworth.

Doll R. (2004) Mortality in relation to smoking: 50 years of observations on male British doctors. *British Medical Journal* 328: 1519.

Enoch, S., Shaaban, H. and Dunn, K .W. (2003) Informed consent should be obtained from patients to use products (skin substitutes) and dressings containing biological material. *Journal of Medical Ethics*, 31, 2-6.

Erzinger, S. (1994) Empowerment in Spanish: 'words can get in the way.' *Health Education Quarterly*, 21, 417-419.

Ethics Department of Catholic Health East (2004) *Patient Preferences: Discrimination in Health care* www.che.org

Fiske J. (1990) *Introduction to Communication Studies*, 2nd edition. London: Routledge.

Giddens, A. (2001) Sociology 4th Ed. Cambridge, Polity

Gillborn, D. (1990) *'Race', Ethnicity and Education: Teaching and Learning in Multi-Ethnic Schools*. London: Unwin.

Gillborn, D. (2005) Educational policy as an act of supremacy: critical race theory and educational reform. *Journal of Educational Policy*, 20, 485-505.

Griffiths, J. and Hope, T. (2000) Access to Sociology: Stratification and Differentiation, London, Hodder and Stoughton.

Goffman, E. (1963) *Stigma: Notes on the Management of Spoiled Identity*. London: Penguin Books.

Goleman, D. (1995) *Emotional Intelligence*. New York, Bantam Books.

Gorham, M. (1989) Spirituality and problem solving with seniors. *Perspective* 13, 13-16.

Gundara, J. (1986) *Racism, Diversity and Education*. London, Hodder and Stoughton.

Hall, S. (1992) New Ethnicities in J. Donals and A. Rattansi (eds) Race, Culture and Difference, London: Sage
/ Open University Press.

Haralambos, M and Holborn, M. (2004) Sociology, Themes and Perspective, sixth edition, London, Collins Education.

Hardie, G.E. (2000) Ethnic descriptors used by

African-American and white asthma patients during induced broncho-constriction. *Chest*, 11, 935-943.

Helman C.G. (1997) *Culture Health and Illness* 3rd Edition. Oxford: Butterworth-Heinemann.

Hicks, W. (1981) *Minorities: A Teacher's Resource Book for Multi-Ethnic Education*. London: Heinemann.

Hume, D. (1753) Essays and treatises on several subjects, Volume 1, London.

Hicks, S (2000) *Four Types of Racism*. http://www.social policy.ca

Illich, I. (1975) *Medical Nemesis*. London: Calder and Boyars.

Kaur, N.(2001) Culturally Competent Care, A good practice guide for care management, Kent, Kent County Council Social Services.

Keesing, R.M. (1981) *Cultural Anthropology*. New York: Holt, Rinehart & Winston.

Kennedy, M. (2010) BNP changes all-white constitution and ejects Times reporter from meeting, London, The Sunday Times, February 14, 2010

Kiev, A. (1964). *Magic, Faith and Healing*. New York: Simon and Schuster.

King, Robert C. and William D. Stansfield (1990), A Dictionary of Genetics. New York: Oxford University Press.

King's College London (2006) *Diabetes Mellitus*. London: King's College Fund.

Koranteng, N.O. (2008) Akaaba, Welcome to Ghana, Twi for Tourist, Acra- Ghana, Combert Impressions

Kush I.K. (1983) *What They Never Told You in History Class*. New York: D and D Distributers Inc.

Kuyvenhoven, M. (1999) Do doctors pay attention

to the religious beliefs of their patients? A survey among Dutch GPs. *Family Practice* 17, 230-232.

Lago, C. (2006) *Race, Culture and Counselling: The Ongoing Challenge*. Maidenhead: The Open University Press.

Laverack, G. (2004) *Health Promotion Practices: Power and Empowerment*. London: Sage Publications.

Legal Eagle Eye Newspapers for the Nursing Profession (1996) *Blood Transfusion: Court Upholds Jehovah's Witness's Right to Refuse*. www.nursinglaw.com

Leonardo, Z. (2002) The souls of white folk: critical pedagogy, whiteness studies, and globalization discourse, *Race Ethnicity and Education*, 5, 29–50.

Little J. (2000) Jehovah's Witnesses drop transfusion ban. London, BBC NEWS,

Lyttle J. (1986) *Mental Disorder: Its Care and Treatment*. Bailliere: London.

MacDonald, I. (1989) *Murder in the Playground: An Inquiry into Racial Violence In Manchester Schools*. London: Longsight Press.

Macionis, J.J. and Plummer, K. (2008) Sociology: A Global Introduction 4ed., Essex, Pearson Education Limited

MacPherson, W. (1999) *The Stephen Lawrence Inquiry*. London: HMSO.

Madhubuti, H. (2009) *Liberation Narratives*. Chicago: Third World Press.

Miller, D (2002) *An Introduction to Jamaican Culture for Rehabilitation Services Providers*. Buffalo, NY: CIRRIE, University of Buffalo.

Moller M. D. and Murphy M.F. (2002) *Recovering from Psychosis: A Wellness Approach* (15th ed.). Nine Miles Falls, WA: Psychiatric Resource

Network.

Morrissey, M. (1998) Applying the Mims-Swenson sexual health model to nurse education: offering an alternative focus on sexuality and health education. *Nurse Education Today*, 18, 488-495.

Morton, E. (2002) Race and racism in the works of David Hume. *Journal of African Philosophy*, 1, 1-20.

Oppenheimer, S. (2006) *The Origins of the British: A Genetic Detective Story*. London: Constable.

Owen, J. (2009) London witchcraft murder linked to African child. *National Geographic News*, December 8th.

Papadopoulos I. and Lees S. (2004) Cancer and communication: similarities and differences of men with cancer form six different ethnic groups. *European Journal of Cancer Care* 13, 154-162.

Parsia, B. (2005) *Understanding Ontologies*. ClarkParsia: Thinking Clearly http://clarkparsia.com

Parks, C.M. (1971) Psycho-social transition: a field for study. *Social Science and Medicine*, 5, 101 -115.

Perry A. G. and Potter, P.A. (2004) Clinical Nursing Skills Technique, USA, Mosby Inc

Pettigrew, T. (1979) The ultimate attribution error: extending Allport's cognitive analysis of prejudice. *Personality and Social Psychology Bulletin*, 5, 461-476.

Pettigrew, T. (2000) Systemizing the predictors of prejudice. In D. Sears (Ed.). *Racialized Politics: The Debate About Racism in America*. Chicago, IL: University of Chicago Press.

Platt, L. (2009) *Ethnicity and Family: Relations Within and Between Ethnic Groups*. Colchester:

Institute of Social and Economic Research, University of Essex.

Polonosky W.H. and Jackson R.A. (2004) What's so tough about taking insulin? Addressing the problem of psychological insulin resistance in type 2 diabetes. *Clinical Diabetes*, 22, 147–150.

Pratt R.J. (2003) *HIV & AIDS, A Foundation for Nursing and Health care Practice* 5th Edition. London: Arnold Publishers

Rack P. (1982) *Race, Culture and Mental Health Disorder*. London: Tavistock Publications

Remen R.N (1999) *On Defining Spirit*.www.parkridgecenter.org, The Park Ridge Centre for Health, Faith and Ethics

Ridley C.R. (1995) *Overcoming Unintentional Racism in Counselling and Theory – A Practitioner Guide To Intentional Intervention*. London: Sage Publications.

Rowntree Trust (2009) *Combining Diversity with Common Citizenship*. York: The Joseph Rowntree Charitable Trust.

Salovey, P. and Mayer, J.D. (1990) Emotional intelligence. *Cognition and Personality*, 9, 185–211.

Seignobos, C. (1938). *Test of a History of the Peoples of Europe*, New York: Charles Schribner.

Sanders, J. and Ewart, B. (2005) *Developing Cultural Competence for Health care Professional Through Work Based Learning*. Abingdon: Radcliffe Publishing.

Sharma, S. and Cruickshank, J. (2001) Cultural differences in providing relevant dietary information to British African Caribbean patients. *Journal of Human Nutrition and Diet*, 14, 449-456.

Sheikh N. and Thomas J. (1994) Factors influencing food choice among ethnic minority adolescents.

Nutrition & Food Science 94, 18-22.

Singh G (1993) *Equality and Education*. Derby: Albrighton Publications.

Solomon, J. (1993) Race and Racism in Britain, 2nd Ed. Macmillan, London

Spardley, J. and McCurdy, D. (1974) Editors' Introduction. In *Conformity and Conflict: Readings in Cultural Anthropology*. Boston: Little, Brown

Spiritus Temporis (2005) Multiculturalism, http://www.spiritus-temporis.com/multiculturalism/official-multiculturalism.html

Strand, S. (2008) *Special Educational Needs and Ethnicity: What we Know*. Warwick: Institute of Education, University of Warwick.

Strawbridge, W. (1997) Frequent attendance at religious services and mortality over 28 days. *American Journal of Public Health* 87, 957-961.

Taylor C. (2004) Social and cultural barriers to diabetes prevention. *Oklahoma America Indian Woman,* 1, no. 2, April.

Teijlingen, E. Van (2003) Maternity satisfaction studies and their limitations. *Birth*, 30, 75-82.

Thompson N. (2003) *Communication and Language: A Hand Book of Theory and Practice*. London: Palgrave Macmillan.

Triandis, H. (1977). *Handbook of Cross-Cultural Psychology*. New York: Brooks-Cole Publishing.

Underwood, A. and Underwood. B. (1981) New spells for old: expectation and realities of Western medicine in a remote tribal society in Yemen, Arabia. In Stanley, N.F. and Joshe, R.A. Eds *Changing Disease Pattern and Human Behaviour*. London, Academic Press.

US Department of Health and Human Services (1999) *Mental Health: A Report of the Surgeon*

General, Rockville, MD: US. Department of Health and Human Services, Center for Mental Health Services, National Institute of Health.

UWA (1997) *Inclusive Curriculum at UWA*. University of Western Australia.

Varcarolis, E. (2006) *Foundations of Mental Health Nursing*. 5th Edition. Cambridge: Elsevier.

Vassel, B. (2004) *Learning, Teaching and Raising Standards:Differentiation Considered*. Birmingham City University, Unpublished.

Vassel, N. (2006) *Diversity and Mental Health Poetry*.
Wolverhampton, privately published.

Verma G.K. (1986) *Ethnicity and Educational Achievement in British Schools*. London: MacMillan Press.

Verma G.K. and Ashworth B (1986) *Ethnicity and Educational Achievement in British Schools*. London: MacMillan.

Vyas, H.V. (1983) Gujaratis in Britain: adaptation and assertion. *Gujarat Samachar*, 13th May 1983.

Williams, J. and Weed, N. (2004) Race and color: relative user ratings. *Assessment*, 11, 316-329.

Yates, J.W. (1981) Religion in patients with advanced cancer, *Medical and Pediatric Oncolology*, 9, 121-126.

Yurugu, M. A (1994) Critique *of European Cultural Thought and Behavior*. N.J: Africa World Press.

Wanless, P. (2006) *Getting it Right: Multicultural Relations in British Schools*. London: HMSO.

WHO (1986) *Ottawa Charter for Health Promotion*. Geneva: World Health Organisation.

Wilson A.N. (1990) Black *on Black Violence: The Psychodynamics of the Black Self Annihilation in Service of White Domination*. New York: Africkan World Infosystems.

Printed in Great Britain
by Amazon.co.uk, Ltd.,
Marston Gate.